THAI WOMEN IN BUDDHISM

THAI WOMEN IN BUDDHISM

CHATSUMARN KABILSINGH

Parallax Press
Berkeley, California

Printed in the United States of America

Parallax Press
P.O. Box 7355
Berkeley, CA 94707

ISBN 0-938077-84-8

Library of Congress Catalog Card #91-42293

Cover Design by Gay Reineck
Text layout adapted from a design by Ayelet Maida
Book composed on a Macintosh IIcx by Lawrence K. Barden

Contents

Preface ix

Foreword xi

CHAPTER ONE Buddhism in Thai History 1

CHAPTER TWO Perspectives on Thai Women 13

CHAPTER THREE Buddhist Texts from a Feminist Perspective 22

CHAPTER FOUR Mae Jis 36

CHAPTER FIVE Two Bhikkhuni Movements in Thailand 45

CHAPTER SIX Nuns' Communities 55

CHAPTER SEVEN Prostitutes and Buddhism 67

CHAPTER EIGHT Buddhist Nuns in Other Countries 87

Bibliography 111

Additional Resources 114

This book is dedicated to my Father, the late Ven. Kokiat Shatsena, who gave me a sense of social justice, expressed primarily through his life—his joy in loving and caring for others. He was the first Thai man I knew who strongly supported the revival of the *Bhikkhuni Sangha* in Thailand.

Preface

When I was just ten years old, my mother became a nun. Rather than following the traditional practice of leaving home, she made our home into a temple. As a result, I grew up as a "temple girl," receiving training and practice like all the nuns in residence. After high school, I studied in India and Canada, and on my return to Thailand, I began teaching at Thammasat University. For many years, I kept these two worlds apart — my academic life and my Buddhist practice.

It was not until 1983, when I was invited to present a paper at Harvard University on "Women, Religion, and Social Change," that I realized the necessity of merging these two worlds. If I know something about the problems that face Thai women in Buddhism and say nothing about them, my knowledge is useless. So I began writing and speaking publicly about this issue, and this book is the fruit of these endeavors. In 1984, I started the *Newsletter on International Buddhist Women's Activities (NIBWA)* which now has readers in thirty-eight countries. As you can imagine, my outspokenness is not at all appreciated at home in Thailand, but this is a vitally important issue that must be discussed.

Although the great majority of the Thai population is Buddhist, the study of religion in my country has long been the prerogative of the Buddhist clergy. Buddhist studies, in the Western academic sense, are new to Thailand. The present work provides the historical background of Buddhism in Thailand and a picture of Thai women in their cultural and historical context. This work focuses on nuns, who are a spiritual reflection of Buddhist society, not only contemporary nuns, but also those who struggled to establish the nucleus of a Bhikkhuni Sangha. Chapter Seven, on "Prostitutes and Buddhism," looks at the contemporary problem of prostitution in Thailand by examining Buddhist attitudes toward prostitutes since the Buddha's time, and deals with how Buddhism can and should provide a stabilizing and uplifting influence in society. The background for Buddhist nuns in other traditions and countries is also provided to give the reader a global context by which to compare and contrast the situation in my country.

This book, a collection of papers written between 1983 and 1990, is the first on the subject of Thai women in Buddhism published in any language. As a pioneer work, it is far from perfect or complete, but I offer it in the hope that it will encourage further research. The work begun here needs to be continued by other scholars from various disciplines, so that the problems being faced by Thai and other women can be alleviated, and we can move in the direction of a better society and a more balanced world.

ACKNOWLEDGMENTS

I am thankful to Thammasat University for granting me a one-year sabbatical, from November 1989 to October 1990, to concentrate on these materials and assemble them as a book. I am also grateful for the valuable help of Martin Perenchio, my American colleague at Thammasat, who spent long hours going through the first draft of my work and discussing points of disagreement; Arnold Kotler, Parallax Press' publisher, a Dharma friend who kindly offered to undertake the publishing of this book; and Marianne Dresser, the editor who made the text presentable to our readers.

Chatsumarn Kabilsingh
August 1991
Bangkok, Thailand

Foreword

This informative new book represents important developments in the study of Buddhism and in the growing body of scholarship about women in Buddhism. It is the first book on women in Thai Buddhism in any language. And it is one of the few books on women and Buddhism to be written by an Asian woman. I join the author in her hope that her endeavors will help end "the 'closed door' policy towards women's full participation in Buddhism in Thailand." Additionally, I would add that I hope her book serves a similar function for women's full participation in all forms of Buddhism.

As the author demonstrates, Buddhism has a long history in Thailand and is thoroughly integrated into Thai culture. Buddhism originally included a strong community of female monastics, but this feature of early Buddhism is lacking in Thai Buddhism. Everyone knows that much, but few know of the negative Thai cultural attitudes toward women that sanction such an omission. Even fewer know of the ways in which women have coped with their exclusion, by forming alternate renunciant communities, even though women in these orders do not receive formal ordination and suffer from many liabilities and prejudices. Fewer still have even thought about the possible links between the absence of the nuns' order in Thai Buddhism and the alarmingly high rate of prostitution in that country, a topic of considerable concern to many. The provocative chapter on "Prostitutes and Buddhism" explores this little-discussed topic in insightful and informative ways.

The information about women in Buddhism in Thailand contained in this book is much more detailed than that found in any other source. That alone makes this book valuable to anyone interested in Buddhism, Thailand, or women's studies.

This book is important, not only for the information it contains, but because its author is an Asian woman. Very little scholarship on women in Buddhism exists. But, almost entirely, what scholarship there is has been written by Western women interested in Buddhism, or by Western women who have become Buddhists. This is espe-

cially the case for the feminist interpretations of Buddhism that are
being done by a few Western Buddhist women. As the author herself notes, "[a]nyone who has studied Western Buddhism cannot
help but notice the uniqueness of women's participation in American Buddhism. American Buddhist women are not only supportive
but also assertive in the role they play in Buddhism."

To date, much of the push for "women's full participation in Buddhism" has come from Western women, even in Asian countries.
While this phenomenon can be explained, both historically and so-
ciologically, by the fuller development of feminism and women's
equality in the West, the situation is untenable in the long run.
Western Buddhist women can and should formulate a Western Buddhism in which women participate fully, and that Western Buddhism may be a helpful model and resource for Asian Buddhist
women. But, in the long run, the movement for women's full participation in Buddhism in Asian Buddhist countries must be led by
Asian women. For this reason, I laud Chatsumarn Kabilsingh's efforts to educate her countrymen about both the history and the
plight of Buddhist women in their own country. Her efforts to dem-
onstrate to them that Buddhist teachings do not support their treatment of the Buddhist women in their midst is even more important.
Perhaps they will listen to what a Buddhist woman from their own
country, who is well educated in Buddhist thought, has to say about
women in Buddhism. She cannot be dismissed as just another West-
erner criticizing Asian culture.

Not only is this book informative and important. It is also inspiring. Many stories about courageous Buddhist women who try to take
their rightful place in Buddhism are found in its pages. Not the least
of these is the story of Chat's mother, who founded the first Buddhist
temple run by and for women in Thailand. I will not forget my time
with them at their temple in Nakhonpathom. Chat says little about
herself in this book. But she too is part of that story of courageous
and inspiring women. It is lonely and frustrating to have so much
that is important, and so few people who are willing to listen. Even
for me, a Western Buddhist feminist, this is quite true. Yet Chat continues her work, year after year, teaching both lay and monastic students, writing and doing research, and organizing and participating

in influential international conferences of Buddhist women, such as the nuns' conference at Bodh Gaya in 1987 and the first international conference of Buddhist women, held in Bangkok in 1991.

Rita M. Gross
Professor, Comparative Studies in Religion
University of Wisconsin, Eau Claire
President, Society for Buddhist-Christian Studies

CHAPTER ONE

Buddhism in Thai History

Thailand has had four historical periods: Sukhothai (1253-1350); Ayudhya (1350-1767); Thonburi (1767-1782); and Ratnakosin (1782-present). The history of Buddhism in Thailand and the history of Thailand as a nation are closely aligned.

Before accepting Buddhism, the Thai people practiced a kind of animism, believing in the spirits of trees, mountains, and other natural phenomena. An important stone inscription dating from the Sukhothai period provides evidence that Thais venerated *Pra Kha P'ung P'i*, the spirit of a mountain, as the greatest spirit in the land and made sacrifices to him in order to gain favor and protection.[1] Later, Buddhism and Indian social values became the norm.

SUKHOTHAI PERIOD (1253-1350)

The earliest evidence of a strong and unified Thai kingdom, with its capital at Sukhothai, dates from the year 1253. By the end of the thirteenth century, the new kingdom had succeeded in driving out the Khmer and Mon peoples and had established control over a vast area in north-central Thailand. For nearly a century, this kingdom began the development of Thai civilization, adopting and synthesizing elements from neighboring cultures and forging its own traditions and customs. Many scholars consider the Sukhothai period the "cradle of Thai culture."[2] The Thai alphabet was developed out of Pali and Sanskrit sources and rendered through Khmer (Cambodian) culture during this period. Khmer aesthetic forms in art and architecture were also adopted.

The Sukhothai period reached its height with the reign of King Ramkhamhaeng (1283-1317), who strengthened the system of benevolent patriarchal rule begun by his father, King Sri-Indraditya, the founder of the Sukhothai kingdom. Ramkhamhaeng's subjects referred to him as "Father," and we are told that he kept in close contact with his people by hanging a bell at his gate that could be sounded by any of his subjects who wanted his attention.[3]

During Ramkhamhaeng's reign, Buddhism enjoyed wide patronage from both the royalty and the common people, both materially
and spiritually. The Buddhist monastic community was divided between *Gamavasi*, those who lived in towns, and *Aranyavasi*, the for-
est-dwellers. Well-known *bhikkhus* (monks) in both divisions
received royal recognition.[4] King Ramkhamhaeng also sent for
learned monks from Sridhammaraja to teach the *Tripitaka*, the Buddhist Canon. *Mahatheras*, senior elders, were invited to preach on
the full and new moon days, and laypersons attended the talks. During the three-month rainy-season retreat, many laypeople congre-
gated to observe the five or eight precepts and make offerings to the
monks.[5] An inscription provides details of such an offering:

> In 1416, there was a celebration of the Great *Stupa* [memo-
> rial monument] *Vihara* [main hall] Buddha-image. The King
> has given 200 acres, the King's mother has given 190 acres.
> Nai Indraksakdi cleared the forest and turned it into a 500-
> acre rice field for the temple.[6]

There is no separate mention of Buddhist women from this period,
and it is understood that there was no ordination for women. Laywomen practiced Buddhism in the same numbers as men, by observing precepts and making offerings to the *Sangha*, the community of
monks. The king invited the elders to preach *Dharma*, the Buddhist
teaching, at public gatherings to which both men and women were
invited, and the king himself also preached publicly. During this
time, *Theravada* Buddhism, the "Way of the Elders," was not the only
religious practice. Although Buddhism was the state religion, indig-
enous animism continued to be popular.

Ramkhamhaeng's grandson, Li Thai, succeeded to the throne in
1346. Well-versed in Buddhist scriptures, Li Thai continued to
strengthen the foundations of Buddhism. He ruled the country in
strict observance of the "Ten Kingly Virtues" proposed in the
Dharmasastra, and made clear his intention to become a buddha
himself in the future to "help his people across the sea of rebirths."[7]
After receiving lower ordination, he announced that he wished for
no treasure of a king, a god, or a Brahma, but only to become a
buddha.[8] These claims are remarkable in light of the usual goals of a

Theravadin Buddhist—that of becoming an *arahat*, "worthy one." To lead the life of a *bodhisattva* was rare, even rarer to aspire to buddhahood. These notions are more common in the *Mahayana* tradition, which must have been popular in Thailand during this time.

Royal participation in Buddhism reached its height when King Li Thai received ordination in 1362. An inscription from 1384 stated that the king was ordained as a *samanera* (novice) in the palace and then went on foot to Wat Pamamuang, Mango Grove Monastery, where he received the bhikkhu ordination.[9] Many others probably followed his example.

The only literary work surviving from the Sukhothai period is the *Tribhumi-gatha*, or *The Treatise of the Three States*, generally believed to have been composed or commissioned by King Li Thai. Drawing on some forty existing texts, this book discusses in detail the three realms according to Buddhism: *kamabhumi*, the realm of pleasure; *rupabhumi*, the realm of form; and *arupabhumi*, the realm of formlessness; and outlines the virtues and vices of those born into each realm. The *Tribhumi-gatha* continued to influence Thai society for many centuries.

The Sukhothai period is often called the Golden Age of Buddhism in Thailand. The high standard of popular and royal spirituality was expressed through practice and in the artistic achievement seen in many fine Buddha images. The firm foundation of Buddhism established during the Sukhothai period provided a stable base for its growth and development during later Thai history.

AYUDHYA PERIOD (1350-1767)

In 1350, a Thai prince from the northern kingdom of Chiengmai established a new capital at Ayudhya. Centered in a productive rice-growing region, at the confluence of three major rivers that formed a naturally fortified site near the Gulf of Siam, Ayudhya benefited from access to communication and local and foreign trade.[10] King Ramathipati I initiated a dynasty that was to span four centuries and thirty-three kings, a period of complex political and social change marked by regular periods of warfare with neighboring kingdoms— Chiengmai and Sukhothai in the north, Khmer in the east, and Burma in the west.

In the reign of Ramesuan (1388-1395), the Khmer capital Angkor Thom was captured, and it was later sacked in 1431 by King Paramaraja II. The Khmer people, driven from the area, withdrew to form present-day Cambodia. During this period of expansion, the Thais absorbed many elements of Khmer culture and synthesized them with Thai customs. Khmer statesmen, religious leaders, and artists played influential roles in the Thai court, affecting its administration and ceremonial and aesthetic forms.

The influence of Brahmanism played a strategic role in the new kingdom, assigning absolute political and religious power in the monarch. The kings in this period did not come to the throne through hereditary succession. There were a great number of royal assassinations, and those who ascended to the throne did so on the basis of power. Brahmanism, by vesting absolute authority in the person of the king,[11] was therefore a potent political tool readily adopted by the new dynasty. Some Brahmanical influence had been felt in the Sukhothai period, but it became the dominant model during the Ayudhya dynasty.

This period was tumultuous, with constant struggles for power from within the kingdom and with neighboring countries. In an environment of political conflict and strife, there was little room for cultural development in the arts, literature, or religion. A drastic change in the structure of government left the royal rulers in complete control of all activities.

Buddhism did not enjoy a solid foundation of royal support as it had in the Sukhothai period. Although it was still the state religion, the Ayudhya monarchy was increasingly influenced by authoritarian Brahmanical tradition, which reinforced the king's status and power. Even the Buddhist institution was used by the king to strengthen and perpetuate his right to rule. Through the manipulation of royal favor and control, the Buddhist order was not able to exert any real influence in secular affairs,[12] and since that time, the Buddhist order has never regained the ability to express any direct concern regarding the political or social welfare of the country.

Ayudhya kings, concerned with maintaining and enlarging their kingdoms, were more involved in warfare with neighboring lands than with developing and strengthening the Buddhist institution.

Their involvement with and support of Buddhism usually took the form of sponsoring religious festivals and commissioning works of art. In addition, famous and beautiful Buddha statues were often among the spoils of war, removed from their original sites after successful military campaigns and installed in the capital city.[13]

King Paramatrailokanath's reign (1441-1481) was the longest of the Ayudhya period. A brilliant administrator, he established a sound system of governmental procedures that became the model for successive periods. In his support of Buddhism, he was Ayudhya's outstanding royal figure. His career in many ways parallels that of the Sukhothai king Li Thai. Paramatrailokanath offered his palace in Pitsanulok, then the capital city, as a temple to the Buddhist community, and he also had another temple built there.[14]

Many outstanding examples of art and architecture date from this period, including Wat Nakhon-luang, modeled on the Khmer capital Angkor Thom. King Narai (1649-1681) constructed a beautiful new city at Lopburi and commissioned many gold- and silver-plated Buddha statues, often on an immense scale.

During the reign of King Th'ai sa (1702-1726), an impressive man-made canal was constructed to allow increased trade with India. The canal required the labor of 30,000 men, supervised by the ex-monk Maha Chai, after whom the canal was named. The king also built a *wat* (temple) called Pa-Mak in Ang-Thong.[15]

Although lacking in direct political power, the Sangha was closely aligned with the state. Secular rulers, including King Paramatrailokanath, joined the order for brief periods. During his reign, seven elders of Chiengmai went to Sri Lanka, where they ordained and studied Dharma and *Vinaya* , the monastic rules, for several years. On their return to Ayudhya, they brought two Sri Lankan senior monks who then founded a new sect, the Wanaratvongsa, named after their teacher. The king, his son, and a nephew all received ordination into this order.[16]

As there was no penalty attached to leaving the Sangha, ordaining for brief periods of time could be used as a refuge from political or military danger. Some ordained monks would leave the order to participate in a war and then rejoin the Sangha whenever they chose.[17] The Sangha was also the primary source of education for many young men.

Many monks also served as teachers and advisors to the king, and their advice was sometimes instrumental in politics. During the reign of Mahathammarajathiraj, when Ayudhya was a vassal state of Burma, the monk Kanchong Mahathera warned Prince Naresuan of an assassination attempt planned by the Burmese, prompting the prince to declare independence from Burma. In another instance, a leading monk intervened when the king ordered the death of some retainers who had abandoned him on the battlefield. And in another incident, as usurpers prepared to take the throne, King Narai had fifty of his loyal retainers ordained, thereby saving them from certain death.

The martial tenor of the Ayudhya period affected the role of the Sangha in Thai society. Young men preparing to go to war sought magical powers to complement their military training, and, naturally, they looked to their teachers, the Buddhist monks, for guidance and support. Ayudhyan monks turned to the study of the *Vedas*, in particular the *Atharvaveda*, to find *mantras*, magical formulas, for the defeat of enemies, and they prepared protective talismans for their followers to wear into battle. These activities were far removed from the teaching of the Buddha, but strength, bravery, and survival, rather than spiritual development, were the primary concerns in the Ayudhya period.

During this period, a synthesis of Brahmanism and Buddhism prevailed in Thailand. Brahmanism had been a part of Thai social and political life since the Sukhothai period, but its influence became more evident from contact with the Khmers during the Ayudhya period. The concept of the ideal king and the "Ten Kingly Virtues" had come to Thailand through the Mon rendering of the *Dharmasastra*. With increased contact with Khmer Brahmanism, the king came to be seen as a divine incarnation—a *devaraja*, god-king. King Narai was believed to be an incarnation of the Hindu god Vishnu; his name is derived from Narayana, the Thai name for that deity.[18]

The royalty and the clergy studied the *Vedas* along with the *Tripitaka*. In prayer before significant acts, kings invoked the names of the Buddha, Shiva, and Vishnu.[19] Court protocol, ceremony, and

Brahmanic values overcome Buddhist values
⟹ enforce ♀'s oppression

administrative systems were based on the Brahmanic model, but in religious life Buddhism retained the higher status. Hindu deities were regarded as subsidiary to the Buddha, subject to impurities and bound to the wheel of rebirths, but in a better position than humans because of their good *karma* (the law of cause and effect, in this case interpreted as rewards or punishments for good or bad things done in this or a previous life).

The Thai people also accepted Brahmanical social and religious values that were repressive to women. The Buddha had attempted to free the spiritual path from the restrictive and negative social values of sixth century B.C.E. India. But centuries later, in Thailand, Buddhist social values were again eclipsed by Brahmanic ethical codes, which restricted women to domestic life, denied them access to education, and subordinated them to male authority and power. Men sought magical powers for the arts of war and also to gain sexual access to women. These values and attitudes towards women were denigrating and lessened women's position in society.

Near the end of Thailand's Ayudhya period, Sri Lanka's King Kittisirirajasiha sent an ambassador and officers to the Thai court requesting help in reviving his country's deteriorating Sangha. King Paramakot sent a group of learned Thai monks to Sri Lanka where they ordained a group of men and established the Siamvongsa sect, which survives to the present day.

THONBURI (1767-1782)

The Thonburi period encompassed the reign of just one king, Tak (Sin), who is rightly considered to be one of the greatest royal figures in Thai history. Although he ruled for only fifteen years, his reign marked an important transition between the violent Ayudhya period and the emergence of modern Thailand.

Ayudhya was sacked and burned by the Burmese in 1761. As many as 200,000 Thais were killed, and the survivors were scattered throughout the country. The Buddhist institutions, centered in Ayudhya, suffered greatly. Most of the wats were razed and burned, many monks were put to death, and Buddhist art treasures were melted down for their gold or silver content or carted off as the spoils of war. Ayudhya had been the political, cultural, and religious cen-

beginnings of a Buddhist revival...

ter of the kingdom, and its loss was devastating.

The dispersed Thai military scattered throughout the country and formed a number of small groups. One such group, led by Sin, gradually gained strength and numbers. An able and courageous leader, Sin led his troops to Ayudhya, and they were able to overthrow the Burmese sovereign and restore the Thai state. Sin became the new king and, leaving the ruined city of Ayudhya, established a new capital at Thonburi. Sin became known as "King Tak the Great."

Tak had received his primary education from a learned monk, and he brought with him to the throne a good understanding of Buddhism. After subduing the residual political unrest, his primary concern was to purify, renew, and strengthen the Sangha. Political upheaval had left a distressed and fragmented society. Ethical standards within the Sangha had deteriorated. King Tak persuaded many dissolute monks to leave the Sangha, including its leader, the *Sangharaja*, "Supreme Patriarch," and he appointed other monks to key positions.[20] He also encouraged many young men to join the Sangha, and he sent learned monks to all the provinces to give instruction to these newly ordained monks. Aware that the complete set of the *Tripitaka* had been lost in the destruction of Ayudhya, he requested copies from the north and the south to be sent to Thonburi for recopying.

During his short reign, Tak proved to be a great monarch and a great protector of Buddhism. His efforts to purify the Sangha and revive Buddhism helped free it from some of the influence of Brahmanism.

RATNAKOSIN (1782-PRESENT)

In 1782, King Yod Fa dethroned Tak and founded the Chakri dynasty. The early years of his reign were consumed with establishing political control in rebellious states, but later he organized the construction of a new capital in Bangkok, Thonburi's sister city. His reign and those of his two successors were dedicated to the reconstruction of the devastated kingdom and reestablishing traditions and customs lost or eroded by the violent upheaval at the end of the Ayudhya period.

During the late nineteenth and early twentieth centuries, increasing contact with the West brought dramatic change to Thailand, and the Thai people had to adjust to the influx of modern ideas and advanced technology. King Rama V (1868-1910) abolished slavery and introduced public hospitals, the beginnings of a national tele-communications system, and many other improvements. In 1932, King Rama VII (1925-1932) introduced a constitutional form of government, thus ending the absolute monarchy. The present king, Bhumipol, took the throne on the sudden death of his brother, King Rama VIII (1934-1946). He has proved himself a devout Buddhist and a popular king.

The purification and revitalization of the Sangha begun during Tak's reign was continued during the Ratnakosin period. Prominent monks who did not meet certain standards were removed from the Sangha, although some continued to serve in the royal offices of King Rama I (1782-1809). Relations with the Sri Lankan Sangha were reestablished during Rama II's reign (1809-1824). The king, disturbed at serious transgressions and degeneration in the Sangha, commissioned from the Sangharaja a text defining correct codes of behavior for monks and had it distributed to all the monasteries and temples.[21]

Prince Mongkut, son of King Rama III (1824-1851), was a devout Buddhist who was ordained in the Sangha. Mongkut was disturbed by the unbecoming behavior of many monks, and after many years of studying the *Pali Canon*, he formed a new sect called *Thammayutika*, "Adherence to the Doctrine." Influenced by the Sri Lankan tradition reestablished under Rama II, the Thammayutika sect was distinguished from the existing Sangha, which became known as the *Mahanikaya*, "Majority Sect." Mongkut's sect was objectionable to many, including his own father, the king, because it followed a foreign model.[22]

Thammayutika monks were known for their moral conduct and seriousness in adhering to the *Vinaya*. Although more conservative in this regard, the sect was more liberal in its approach to interpreting Dharma. Religious services were conducted in the vernacular to enable the people to follow and understand.[23] Thammayutika monks stressed the importance of making the teaching meaningful and accessible to all.

improvement in $'s status

When he ascended the throne in 1851, Mongkut took care not to favor his reform sect over the established Sangha.[24] But the Thammayut monks did receive more positions in the Sangha hierarchy, however, because they tended to be better educated. Since they were the minority sect, this caused some tension between the two sects. Recently the situation has improved, with Mahanikaya monks' increased interest in scholarship. There are now two Buddhist universities in Bangkok, one for each sect.

The purification of the Sangha in the early Ratnakosin period removed much of the remaining Brahmanical influence from Buddhism. With this, the status and position of women in Thai society began to improve. Women were allowed greater access to education. Saobhava, the queen of King Rama V, strongly supported the establishment of educational institutions for girls.

The custom of royal ordination that began in the Sukhothai period was reestablished in the Ratnakosin period by King Rama I, who had his son ordained for one rainy-season retreat. This prince later ascended the throne as Rama II.[25] Prince Mongkut had been in the order for twenty-seven years when he ascended the throne, and he also had his son, Prince Chulalongkorn, ordained as a novice.[26] As King Rama V, Chulalongkorn continued the tradition by having his son ordained. One of his younger brothers became a learned monk and later Sangharaja, many of whose written works became texts studied by monks in later periods. The present king and the Crown Prince also joined the order for a short time, studying the *Tripitaka* and practicing meditation. In continuing this tradition, King Bhumipol has set an example to the Thai people and helped strengthen the connection between the Sangha and the Thai monarchy.

King Rama II was concerned about the observance of religious days, which had been discontinued during the last years of the Ayudhya period. After consulting with the Sangharaja, he reestablished the national observance of *Visakha*, the birthday of the Buddha, a three-day period during which the King himself observes eight precepts, honors the Sangha, and performs other pious acts. He also requested a religious ceremony to help drive away an outbreak of cholera, and again observed precepts during the crisis. According

King ⟷ Sangha

Western influences have lessened importance of B.
for the Thai people
Buddhism in Thai History

to tradition, the disease was contained in fifteen days.

Rama IV introduced a corollary to the custom that began in Ayudhya in which princes and officers swore their fidelity to the king. The king, in turn, pledged his loyalty to the people, and this custom continues to the present day. All important Buddhist holy days are now national holidays, observed by the Thai royalty. The king personally attends the seasonal changing of the Emerald Buddha's robes in the Royal Temple in Bangkok.

The relationship between the king and the Sangha is mutually supportive. The king pays respect to the Sangha as representative of moral and religious discipline, and as a gesture of respect to the Buddhist tradition as a whole. The appointment of the Sangharaja, in turn, is ultimately granted by the king, based on the suggestions of a group of prominent monks. From the beginning of Thai history, the Buddhist Sangha has depended on the support of the ruling aristocracy. It is part of the king's role to protect and uphold Buddhism. The kings of the present dynasty continue to fulfill this role.

Buddhism in Thailand has undergone many stages in its development and has been molded by a variety of influences. From its strength in the Sukhothai period, to the violent upheavals in the Ayudhya period, to the revitalization in the Ratnakosin period, the most crucial problem Thai Buddhism faces today does not result from any lack of political support, but from the negligence of those within the tradition itself. The educational system often fails to impart a fundamental knowledge of Buddhism to the Thai people. With the arrival of modern technology and Western ways, the teachings of Buddhism have begun to seem irrelevant and meaningless to many. Many people do not feel the need to develop themselves spiritually or seek the ultimate goal of Buddhist practice, enlightenment. They are satisfied to concentrate on material pursuits.

There is an urgent need for the Buddhist institution in Thailand to reframe the teachings in an understandable and relevant manner for the present situation, and most importantly, to provide increased access to the study and practice of Buddhism to all members of Thai society. If this approach is adopted, the teachings of the Buddha will once again become meaningful for the Thai people, men and women equally.

[1] *Sukhothai stone inscription no. 1.* Translated by Cham Thongkhamwan (Bangkok: Ramkhamhaeng University, 1971).

[2] Horace Geoffrey Quaritch Wales, *Early Burma - Old Siam* (London: Bernard Quaritch, 1973), p. 2.

[3] King Ramkhamhaeng's inscription pillar no. 1, *The Inscription of King Ramkhamhaeng the Great* (Bangkok: Chulalongkorn University, 1984).

[4] Thanom Anamwat, et al., *Thai History* (Bangkok: Amara Karnpim, 1975), p. 82.

[5] *Sukhothai stone inscription no. 1*, p. 90.

[6] Wat Sorasak inscription no. 8, *The Inscription of King Ramkhamhaeng the Great* (Bangkok: Chulalongkorn University, 1984).

[7] Wat Pamamuang inscription no. 5, *The Inscription of King Ramkhamhaeng the Great* (Bangkok: Chulalongkorn University, 1984), side 1, lines 4-33.

[8] Wat Pamamuang inscription no. 4, side 2, lines 494-51.

[9] *Ibid.*

[10] Anamwat, *Op. Cit.*, p. 128.

[11] Wales, *Op. Cit.*, p. 5.

[12] *Ibid.*, p. 6.

[13] Pra Bariharndepathani, *The Thai History* (Bangkok: Prajavidya, 1968), Vol. II, p. 144.

[14] Pra Chomklao, ed., *Pongsawadan* (Bangkok: Mahamakut Press, 1952), Vol. I, part 1, p. 419.

[15] Anamwat, *Op. Cit.*, p. 145.

[16] *Tamnan Yonok*, quoted in *Pongsawadan*, Vol. 1, part 1, p. 429.

[17] Manich Jumsai, *Popular History of Thailand*, p. 256.

[18] U. Pramounvidya, *In the Palace of King Narai Maharaja* (Bangkok, 1962), p. 507.

[19] Pramounvidya, *Op. Cit.*, p. 396.

[20] Sangharaja Di, Sangharaja Sri, *Pongsawadan*, Vol. II, part 2, p. 168.

[21] Chaopraya Tipakornwong, *Praraj Pongsawadan Krung Ratnakosin Rachakan II* (Bangkok: Gurusabha Press, 1961), p. 208.

[22] Pra Boromrajchakrivongsa (Bangkok: The Royal Secretariat, 1985), p. 234.

[23] A.B. Griswold, "King Mongkut in Perspective," in *Journal of Siam Society*, Bangkok, Vol. IV, p. 283.

[24] Griswold, *Op. Cit.*, p. 285.

[25] Tipakornwong, *Op. Cit.*, p. 822.

[26] *Ibid.*, p. 386.

Thai ♀ are doubly exploited
↳ class + gender biases

CHAPTER TWO

Perspectives on Thai Women

In order to understand the position and problems of Thai women in Buddhism, it is necessary to examine the social and cultural roles of women generally in Thailand. Historically, the training and social conditioning of Thai women has been aimed at producing "good women" who are well-equipped in the traditional "home sciences"—cooking, carving fruit into beautiful offerings for their husbands, and maintaining the home. It has been accepted for many years that Thai women do not have critical or intellectual capacities, and that women are the "weaker sex," "flowers of the world" to serve and please men.[1]

It is, of course, absurd to say that women are the "weaker sex." In traditional village life, women have always worked side by side in the fields with men. Then, while the men relax after returning from a day of working in the fields, women cook the meals, take care of children, clean, and weave.[2]

During the last thirty years, agricultural failure resulting from backward or inadequate technology has forced many village women to seek employment in urban industrial areas, primarily in the capital, Bangkok. Many textile factories prefer to hire women because they produce better work, are less trouble to control or manipulate, and are paid less than men.[3] Thai women continue to be suppressed in economics, politics, and culture. It is rare to find mention of the endurance and self-sacrifice of Thai women in the pages of my country's history. Women are doubly exploited, both in the class structure of Thai society and in the gender bias within that structure.[4]

EDUCATION

Historically, education for Thai women was based on the above-stated social values of women's roles. Social attitudes significantly shaped and narrowed the educational framework for women, limiting it to one purpose—to mold women to be good housewives.

Lack of educational
opportunities
for ♀ (except aristocracy)

Women's restricted educational opportunities provided them with training only in the "home sciences," effectively barring women from any wider public or social role. Educational methods relied on rote memorization, and women were never encouraged to exercise independent critical thought. The subordinate position of women in Thai society was aptly summed up in the popular expression, "Women are the hind legs of the elephant."

In the Sukhothai period, a text by Lady Srichulalak, a consort of King Ramkhamhaeng, records that women of high social status received the same education as men in literature, drawing, astronomy, and astrology. Common women, however, received no education, primarily because the center for education was the temple. The Buddhist monks taught only male students, because the *Vinaya* forbade them to come into direct contact with women. In the strife of the Ayudhya period, women were not educated except for being trained to become good wives and mothers.

During King Narai's reign (1649-1681), upper-class families sent their daughters to be trained at the palace, which was then the only educational institute for women. But women in general still received limited education. They were restricted from the study of language or literature, in the belief that it would encourage them to write love poetry to men. Nevertheless, two princesses of King Baromkot emerged as talented poets whose literary works have survived to the present. Women courtiers were trained in the arts of classical dance, singing, and drama to fulfill their roles as entertainers to the king.

It was not until 1782 , with the advent of the Ratnakosin period, that Thai women began to have greater opportunities for higher education, although it was still largely limited to royal families and their associates. This period saw an increasing exposure to the West, coinciding with the relative freedom from Brahmanical influence in the reign of King Rama IV. His son, Prince Damrong, recorded that between the ages of three and seven princes and princesses were educated together. After this identical primary education, princesses would then receive separate training in the home sciences. In higher education, they received instruction in various fields such as religion, literature, and history.

During the reign of Rama IV (1851-1868), some progress was made in education for women, although it continued to be restricted to those from the upper classes. Female missionaries from abroad, or the wives of male missionaries, were hired to teach young girls of the court. For the first time, Thai women went abroad for further education. Young girls from upper-class families were educated at court along with the daughters of the royal families. Thailand's first female teacher, Princess Pichitjirabha, founded Rajini, a well-known girls' school.

Queen Saovabhapongsi ruled as acting regent during King Rama V's travels abroad. She recognized the growing demand by women to receive equal educational opportunities, not to compete with men but to better equip them for their accepted social role, especially because they had to teach their children.

Women began to receive university-level education in 1927, with the founding of Chulalongkorn University. Its first students were seven women studying both the arts and sciences. Although active for only ten years, Chulalongkorn University established a precedent for higher education for women; since its time slow but steady progress in university education for women has been made. However, even as late as 1952 only a small percentage of Thai girls were eligible to continue their education beyond the primary level, compared to the majority of Thai boys.

With small advances in education, a few of the baseless negative beliefs that for centuries obstructed women's development are diminishing. But most negative gender biases are still fully operative in Thai society.

THAI WOMEN AND THE LAW

The subordinate position of women in Thai society was formally maintained in its legal system. Women were explicitly assigned responsibilities and duties, while granted very few rights. Early Thai law was heavily influenced by Brahmanism and its vigorous repression of women. In the Sukhothai period, three sources directly influenced Thai legal structure: the *Manu Dharmasastra*, the *Arthavaveda*, and the Buddhist teachings. The Indian social norms these sources represented were repressive for women in greater or lesser degrees and formed the basis of Thai social norms and law. In the *Vinaya Pitaka Mahavibhanga*, women were categorized as property, subject to the dominance and protection of either their husbands or other male family members. Wives (and children) could be sold to repay a loan according to the *Mangrai Sastra*.[5] Northern Thailand's *Lanna* law placed the material value of a girl as exactly half that of a boy.[6] Matrimonial law during King Uthong's time was based on the *Dharmasastra*, which says that a husband legally owns his wife and can beat her with impunity, as one might beat a recalcitrant farm animal.[7] As recently as the eighteenth century, with the establishment of the Ratnakosin dynasty, King Rama I still used the *Dharmasastra* as a model for new legal standards.

At last, King Rama IV said that the old law was unjust, that it treated "women as buffalo, men as human beings."[8] He introduced a code of law that forbade a man from selling his wife unless she agreed to it; however, he could sell her if she was a slave. A man could still legally beat his wife, but if she were seriously harmed he could be fined.[9] His code also established that a woman could choose her own husband after coming of age.[10]

Since that time, Thai society has changed a great deal. From being primarily agricultural and village-based, it has become semi-industrial. Women now participate more fully in economic production and, with better education, the role of women in Thai society has substantially improved, and the laws reflect these changes. In 1974, equal rights for men and women were established.[11] King Rama VI wrote that equal legal rights are a mark of a civilized society.[12]

It has often been noted that Thai women seem to accept their suppression without complaint. Exploitation, whether physical, legal, or cultural, has been justified on the basis of karma, and has therefore been accepted as the expression of religious principle. Although Thai women have always hoped to be treated well by their husbands, until recently few had the intellectual training necessary to examine the social, economic, and political factors informing the discrimination that ruled their lives.

In 1948, the Universal Declaration of Human Rights declared that men and women are equal in their rights and honor.[13] In 1967, the United Nations disestablished any practice or tradition based on the suppression or exploitation of women, and it later declared 1975 the "International Year of Women."[14] The Thai government responded by lifting restrictions on female lawyers in the courts, establishing the right of Thai women to travel abroad with or without permission from their husbands, and allowing women to hold leadership positions in village societies.

Professor Malee Pruegpongsawalee, a well-known Thai lawyer and educator, has pointed out that legal equality is a necessary prerequisite for women to fully participate in building the Thai nation.[15] The attempt to bring about equal rights is not only for the benefit of women, but to help the country realize the potential contribution of half its population. In order to develop human resources to their fullest, the Thai government must abandon biased legal structures that obstruct this goal.

THAI WOMEN AND POLITICS

Thai women had the right to vote earlier than some European women, but due to lack of education concerning the democratic process, their right to vote carried little political weight. It was not until 1949 that the first female member of parliament was elected. In 1979, nine women were elected to parliament out of 301 seats, and this was the highest ratio of female participation to date. As recently as 1981, only fifty-four seats were occupied by women, again representing the greatest number of female members of parliament.

In other areas, such as economics, academia, and health services, women hold a majority of the administrative positions and manifest a strong sense of self-confidence in dealing independently with the challenges presented by their careers. The example of these and other women will help erode the common belief that women are the "hind legs of the elephant," unsuited for public or political life.

However, social values resulting from the belief that "a woman's place is in the home" are still dominant in Thailand. Long denied equal access to higher education, women have not in great numbers received the solid intellectual foundation required to participate fully in political life. Lack of the necessary financial resources needed to conduct successful campaigns also severely limits women's involvement in politics. Although Thai politics have taken a positive turn in the last two decades, the future of women in Thai political life remains uncertain.

THAI WOMEN AND ECONOMIC RESPONSIBILITY

The picture of a man going out to work earning a living to support his family while his wife stays home to take care of the household is outdated. With present-day economic pressures, men and women both bear economic responsibility. Forty-five percent of Thai women work, the highest percentage in Asia. But most are employed as unskilled laborers in low-paying agricultural or industrial work.

Under the system of corvee labor in the Ayudhya period, men would be away from their homes at least every other month, sometimes for as long as three months. During their absence, women took care of the families. Because of this, it was customary for newly married couples to live with the wife's family. This led to a matrilineal social system and also to relative financial independence for women. While big business was in the hands of Chinese traders and foreign trade was under the control of the king, Thai women became quite skillful in small-scale business, earning a degree of financial independence and some business skills.

But agriculture is still the primary work of three-fourths of Thai women, working with their husbands or male relatives. As already noted, rural women who work in the fields also take care of children and manage the household. Eighty-one percent of Thai women age fifteen or older work; the number rises to 87% in the forty-four to forty-nine age group.[16] It is impossible to state in exact percentages the extent to which Thai women provide economic assistance to their families, but it is certain that without women's help, many Thai families would not survive.[17]

In a recent study, it was found that 87.5% of the women interviewed are responsible for managing family finances.[18] Seventy-three percent of rural women felt that the family's income was insufficient for its needs and this was a source of great concern.[19] Eighty-five percent agreed that it was necessary for women to work outside the home to help bring in more income.[20] Women in different regions participate in different types of work. In the north and south, women prefer agricultural work, while women from the central region (especially urban areas) prefer small businesses and service work. Women from the northeast engage in cottage industries, such as weaving.[21]

- different labor preferences/practices
  in different parts of country
- majority of negative perception of ♀ come from
  foreign influences

Perspectives on Thai Women

Private domestic service is not a popular option; only 12% of women from the northeast, Thailand's poorest region, chose such work, while none from the south show any interest in it. This reflects both economic and cultural differences. Southern Thailand is a wealthier region, and to work as a housemaid is not considered desirable there; while people of the northeast more easily accept such work and see it as helping others.

While it is true that Thai women manage the family finances, this does not necessarily lead to economic control. Women may hold the family "purse strings," but in most cases, the purse is empty. Women have no real economic power, but do have the responsibility to make ends meet. This is a major fact of life for most Thai women, both rural and urban.[22]

WOMEN AND SOCIAL PERCEPTIONS IN THAI SOCIETY

Negative perceptions of women, due primarily to extensive Chinese and Indian influence, have had a great impact on Thai society. During King Rama II's reign, when an active trade relationship was developed with China, great numbers of Chinese settled in Thailand, and many Chinese immigrants married Thais. Chinese cultural values were integrated with Thai beliefs. There were five negative characteristics assigned to women in traditional Chinese thought: women are easily manipulated, always unsatisfied, jealous, insulting, and of lesser intelligence. In traditional China, as in so many other societies, the position of women was subordinated to men in social, economic, political, and cultural life on the basis of such definitions.

5 negative ♀ characteristics

As already noted, Indian cultural values to a great extent mirrored these same beliefs: women were always to be under the guidance and protection of the men to whom they were affiliated—as children, to their fathers; as wives, to their husbands; as mothers, to their sons. Women were not seen as independent human beings, but were, like livestock or land, the possessions of men.

In Thailand, men generally have an exploitative attitude towards women. Women born into such a gender-stereotyped society will tend to internalize these beliefs and accept them as valid. Commonly held prejudices of women's mental and physical inferiority, handed down through cultural tradition and sanctioned by religion, have profoundly affected Thai women's self-image and expressions of self-worth. With restricted access to positions of public authority, women have been taught to channel their interests and abilities into such superficial preoccupations as the beauty of their physical appearance, too often the only thing for which they can gain attention. Such social values and mentality will never help women to come forward as individuals.

Some women of the upper classes in Thai society may not experience repression so directly. They may believe that they enjoy equal rights, protected as they are by wealth and social status from the more obvious social and economic hardships. But an oppressive and exploitative mentality ultimately affects everyone, men and women of every class.

In Thailand's fast-changing society, roles today are shaped primarily by economic pressure. Women are beginning to share economic responsibility, and in the process they are gaining greater access to the educational opportunities to prepare them for this expanded role. Women are making their way in fields previously closed to them, becoming successful educators, doctors, lawyers, and businesswomen. These changing roles will definitely bring about a change in social values. But for now, there are many deep-rooted cultural values that continue to restrict women's equal participation in Thai society. Until these are replaced by egalitarian beliefs, Thai women will continue to find themselves unable to express fully their human potential.

---

[1] Kularb Saipradit and Jit Bhumisak, *History of Thai Women* (Bangkok: Somchai Press, 1976), p. 4.

[2] *Ibid.*, p. 127.

[3] *Ibid.*, p. 143.

[4] *Ibid.*, pp. 128-9.

[5] Thanin Kraiwichien, *Women's Right in Thai Law* (Bangkok: Government House Press, 1967), p. 2.

[6] Virada Somsawat, *Women and Social Reality* (Bangkok: Rungwathana Press, 1980), p. 75.

[7] *Ibid.*, p. 86.

[8] *Ibid.*, p. 2.

[9] *Blossoming Movement*, Female Students Group, Chulalongkorn University (Bangkok: Chareonvit Press, 1973), p. 35.

[10] Saipradit and Bhumisak, *Op. Cit.*, p. 108.

[11] Bavorn Prapuetdee, et al., *Role of Thai Women in Administration* (Bangkok: Thaikasem, 1977), p. 71.

[12] *Blossoming Movement*, p. 35.

[13] Sudarat Supbhibat, *Sexual Exploitation of Thai Women* (Bangkok: Chareonvit Press, 1984), p. 176.

[14] U.N. Declaration no. 3010 (XXVII), January 7, 1973.

[15] Malee Pruegpongsawalee, "Why Legal Equality Is Necessary for Development" (Unpublished paper, Thammasat University, Bangkok, 1982), p. 196.

[16] Nanthana Chaiyasut, ed., *Report on Survey of Status of Women in Two Provinces* (Unpublished report, Bangkok, 1977), p. 26.

[17] *Ibid.*, p. 26.

[18] Santi Komolbutra, trans., *History of Siam*. From *Description royaume de Thai au Siam*, by Fr. Pallegois. (Bangkok: Kaona Press, 1963), p. 27.

[19] *Report on Survey of Problems and Need of Women in Rural Area according to Project on Developing Women* (Bangkok: Ministry of Internal Affairs, Research and Evaluation Department, 1981), p. 16.

[20] *Ibid.*, p. 34.

[21] *Ibid.*, p. 36.

[22] Khunying Dr. Amporn Meesuk, Welcome Address, Asian Regional Workshop on "The Role of Women Contributing to Family Income," July 1976 (Unpublished, supported by Friedrich-Ebert-Stiftung, Bangkok, June 1977), p. 41.

CHAPTER THREE

Buddhist Texts from a Feminist Perspective

Women have shown an interest in following the path to spiritual salvation since the time of the Buddha, nearly 2,600 years ago. They expressed a sincere commitment by dedicating their lives as *bhikkhunis*, fully ordained nuns in the Buddhist order. The recorded histories of many Buddhist countries, such as Sri Lanka and China, offer evidence of the early existence of bhikkhuni orders. Still, despite the ideal in Buddhist thought of the availability of spiritual attainment for all sentient beings without discrimination, within the Buddhist establishment itself opportunities for women to express a genuine commitment to practicing the path have often been restricted.

There is an urgent need for us to examine the obstacles placed before women on the Buddhist path. Through a critical analysis of Buddhist texts, we can determine the ways that women are supported and the ways they are repressed by the institutional structures of Buddhism. Such an examination is not only the province of Buddhist scholars, but can also be carried out by feminist scholars of other religious and cultural backgrounds. Interfaith dialogue among diverse groups of scholars has proven to be of great benefit to Buddhist scholarship.

The First Council of the Sangha, held three months after the Buddha's passing, *Parinirvana*, was attended by five hundred enlightened men. Mahakassapa presided over the Council, with Upali reciting the *Vinaya*, and Ananda reciting the *Sutras*, texts of the Buddha's own words. The *Tripitaka*, the "three baskets" of the teachings, had not yet been formed; the *Abhidharma*, its third section, did not yet exist at the time of the First Council. The teachings agreed upon at this Council were preserved through oral transmission, the practice common at the time.

There are two important points about the First Council regarding women. First, although there were a number of enlightened bhikkhunis, highly praised by the Buddha for their knowledge of the

Vinaya, skill in giving Dharma talks, and attainment in wisdom and spiritual powers,[1] none were invited to the Council. It is tempting to surmise that this may have been due to the prejudices of the Bhikkhu Sangha. A Sri Lankan monk has pointed out that it was regarded as incorrect to recite the *Bhikkhuni Patimokkha*, rules of the nun's order, in the absence of the bhikkhunis.[2]

Second, Ananda was accused by the other monks of having committed an offense by encouraging the Buddha to accept women into the monastic order.[3] Ananda replied, "But I, honored sirs, made an effort for the going forth of women in the Dharma and discipline proclaimed by the Truth-finder, thinking: this Gotami Pajapati... giver of milk, for when the Lord's mother passed away, she suckled him. I do not see that as an offense..."[4] Even though Ananda made it clear that he felt he had committed no wrongdoing, he confessed to the offense in order to save the Sangha from further disagreement and possible schism. This event suggests that, among the hundreds of arahats in the First Council of the Sangha, many strongly opposed the establishment of the Bhikkhuni Sangha. Unable to go against the decision of the Buddha during his lifetime, they raised the issue immediately after his Parinirvana.

The Buddhist texts as we know them today were first written down at least three hundred years after the Buddha's Parinirvana. They were believed to have been preserved in Pali, and it is questionable whether Pali was ever a spoken language. The Buddha spoke Artha-Maghadi, the dialect of Magadha, the region in northeast India where he lived and taught. The *Canon* was written down at a later Council held in Sri Lanka, thousands of miles away from there and from where the earliest Buddhist communities had been located. The authenticity of the *Pali Canon* as the actual words of the Buddha cannot be accepted without question, given these differences in time, language, and location.

The Buddhist texts were recorded by monks. These monks were not necessarily enlightened arahats, and even among the so-called enlightened Sangha at the First Council, we can see evidence of prejudice against women in their exclusion of bhikkhunis from the Council, their treatment of Ananda, and their opposition to the Bhikkhuni Order. The recorders chose to preserve the messages of

2 levels of B. teaching:
1) core - no gender bias
2) general - possible interpretation of biases

THAI WOMEN IN BUDDHISM

the text according to their own subjective standards of what was important.

The Bhikkhu Sangha, whether in the Buddha's time or during succeeding centuries, were men drawn from the social and cultural background of India. It is inevitable that they carried with them, consciously or unconsciously, the values of that culture, which, as noted, were extremely oppressive to women. The caste system, by its very structure, is oppressive not only to women, but to almost everyone. Brahmans, the priestly caste, were largely responsible for establishing social codes of behavior. The *Manu Dharmasastra*, a product of Brahmanism, became the ethical code for later Hindu society in India. Its influence was also felt in neighboring countries influenced by Indian culture. The Buddhist texts were recorded by men drawn from this social structure and its values.

It has often been asked, especially in the West, whether Buddhism is oppressive to women or if it offers a liberating spiritual path for them. It is important for scholars to distinguish between two levels of teaching in the tradition. The first is the core teaching of Buddhism that deals directly with the spiritual path. This level is free from contextual and gender bias by its very nature. The question of bias or oppression is not applicable here, because the Buddha's teachings transcend gender difference. The highest goal of Buddhism is enlightenment, and the spiritual path leading to it is available to all sentient beings, without discrimination.

The second category of the teachings exists on a more mundane level and is indeed affected by social context. At this level, we can find evidence in the texts to support both sides of the argument. The basic teaching of Buddhism rests on the simple fact that everyone goes through the process of birth, decay, and death. Suffering is a common experience. The Buddha professed that everyone has the potential to transcend suffering, but it is up to each individual to pursue this goal. In this basic teaching there is also no room for gender bias. But we do find gender bias within the texts and so we need to examine carefully each passage and its context to discover the origins of the bias.

Despite the fact that the Buddha's teaching defied many existing social and religious values of his time, the Buddha was still very much a part of Indian culture. Evidence reveals how he made certain decisions on practice and rules in alignment with existing values. When Ananda asked whether monks should pay homage to nuns according to seniority, he replied that other spiritual leaders who propounded imperfect doctrines sanctioned homage of women by men, therefore he could not do so.

In her study on women and Buddhism in the *Jatakas*, Boonsue Kornvibha criticized the Buddha for not being entirely free from socially conditioned values, even though he was enlightened.[5] But we must understand that the fully enlightened Buddha was an historic person, born into a specific social and cultural context that influenced his life. He retained some social values that appear to be strongly prejudiced from a modern standpoint. This should be kept in mind as we examine passages from the Buddhist texts.

In the recorded teaching the Buddha is said to have given the monks, he reminds them that "woman is a stain on celibacy."[6] In Thailand this passage is taken quite literally, and monks will not come into direct contact with a woman. Women are looked down upon and viewed as a hindrance to the spiritual development of the monks.

This example reflects how the Buddhist texts are primarily androcentric—male-centered. They were recorded by monks, in the interest of monks. Newly ordained monks who have not had much experience with practice and are very weak in their mental resolve may be easily swayed by sensual impulses, of which women are the major attraction. Even if no women are present, some monks still create problems for themselves by images of women they have in their minds. Women are not responsible for the sexual behavior or imaginings of men; the monks themselves must cope with their own sensual desires. Enlightened ones are well-fortified against such mental states and are able to transcend gender differences. The Buddha himself found no need to avoid women, because women no longer appeared to him as sexual objects. He was well-balanced and in control of his mental processes.

In a conversation with Ananda, the Buddha was recorded to have given advice to the monks regarding contact with women. They were not to look at them and not to spend time talking with them[7]

andeocentric

[Handwritten margin notes at top:]
♀'s negative self-view
⤷ influenced by onesided teachings
presence of Indian social values
→ not necessarily relevant to Thai ♀'s experience

because "nothing binds men as strongly as women."[8] There was a parallel warning for women, but it has been seldom repeated or discussed as the monks were and are the primary teachers of Dharma, so the teaching has been predominantly one-sided in approach. Women have been made to appear as sources of impurity and hindrances to spiritual growth, which undoubtably has negatively affected women's self-view.

Certain passages from the *Canon* clearly convey Indian social values. "Women are the supreme commodity,"[9] reflects the ideas expressed in the *Manu Dharmasastra* that women are precious commodities to be passed on from fathers to husbands to sons. Another passage states that "women are subject to five woes"—that she must leave her family at marriage; that she must suffer the pain of menstruation, pregnancy and childbirth; and that she must always work hard taking care of her husband.[10] Two of these "woes" were social conventions about proper roles and behavior, and three are simply properties of the female body. That menstruation, pregnancy, and childbirth are characterized negatively reflects male biases, fear, and misunderstanding. In Indian culture, women left their families at marriage, an often painful and difficult separation. In Thai society, it was more common for a husband to live with his new wife's family. Therefore, this particular form of suffering, common in the lives of Indian women, bears litle relationship to Thai women's experience. Similarly, characterizing taking care of one's husband as suffering may have been true in the context of Indian culture, but in modern society, marriage requires a commitment from both parties, and taking care of one's spouse can be an enjoyable, positive experience for both. Explaining to Ananda his reservations about women joining his order, the texts quote the Buddha as saying that women are selfish, poor in wisdom, and therefore unable to assume a seat in the assembly, and that they cannot work and cannot travel to distant lands.[11] In such passages, social values and cultural norms specific to a time and place far removed from our own are glaringly apparent.

The oft-repeated statement in the texts that "a woman cannot become a buddha" has been demonstrated by Japanese Buddhist scholar Kajiyama Yuichi to be a late addition to the *Canon*.[12]

26

Kajiyama has distinguished five historical stages regarding the Buddhist attitude toward women's potential for enlightenment:

> 1. Primitive Buddhism under Gautama and his direct disciples made no distinction between men and women with regard to emancipation, despite the prevalence of societal discrimination against women in ancient India.
>
> 2. By comparing various Pali and Chinese sources, it appears that the dictum that a woman is incapable of becoming a Buddha probably arose around the first century B.C.E.
>
> 3. Just before the beginning of the Christian Era, a new movement developed in which Aksobhya Buddha and Amitabha Buddha, sympathizing with the predicament of women, vowed to save them: Aksobhya by removing all physical and social difficulties of women in his Buddha Land; Amitabha by transforming women into men on their birth in his Western Paradise.
>
> 4. Early Mahayana sutras, such as *The Perfection of Wisdom in 8,000 Lines*, the *Lotus Sutra*, and the *Pure Land Sutra*, developed the idea that a woman can be enlightened by transforming herself into a male.
>
> 5. The mature philosophy of emptiness and Buddha nature in all sentient beings, represented in the *Vimalakirti Nirdesa*, *Srimaladevi*, and other sutras, declares that a woman can be enlightened just as she is, as a woman.

In addition, Professor Kajiyama has discussed the belief in the thirty-two physical marks (*mahapurisalaksana*) distinguishing a buddha as a "great man." Since the tenth mark concerns a buddha's "concealed genital," it has been assumed that a buddha must be of the male gender. But another interpretation suggests that the symbolic meaning of a concealed genital is that an enlightened person is no longer at the mercy of sensual appetites. The association of the historical Buddha with the *mahapurisalaksana* of a *cakravartin*, "universal monarch," excluded women from becoming a buddha in the context of Indian society and has unfortunately influenced later social and religious values that deny women's spiritual potential.

There remains the question of the Buddha's hesitation to allow women admission into the Sangha. According to the texts, the

author considers both sides of argument ♂ ♀ in Sangha
→ considers historical + cultural context

Buddha repeatedly refused Mahapajapati Gotami, his aunt and step-mother, when she approached him for admission to the Sangha. This has often been interpreted as proof that the Buddha was against the idea of women leading religious lives. However, the Buddha may have had practical considerations for discouraging Mahapajapati Gotami and the hundreds of royal women who followed her. Leaving a life of privilege and comfort for the rigors of the ascetic spiritual path of early Buddhism would have been difficult. Nonetheless, the Buddha acknowledged the determination and sincerity of these women, who followed him from village to village repeating their request to join his order.

Other factors influenced the Buddha's decisions regarding the Bhikkhuni Sangha, for instance the question of residence and teachers. Early Buddhists were "forest-dwelling" mendicants. Such a solitary, unprotected life was dangerous for women; there was a case of a bhikkhuni being raped.[13] Another problem arose around the availability of qualified teachers. In the *Vinaya*, it is stated that only qualified monks appointed by the Sangha could teach bhikkhunis. Bhikkhunis, before asking a monk any questions on the Buddhist teaching, had to first determine if he was qualified to teach.[14]

The texts state that after admitting women into the Sangha, the Buddha imposed a set of eight additional rules that they were to follow. These Eight Important Rules, the *Gurudharma*, have often been cited by Western scholars as proof (by current standards) of a negative gender bias in Buddhism. They range from requiring senior nuns to pay homage to new monks (a rule that reverses the usual hierarchy of seniority in the Sangha), to stipulating that a nun must never speak badly of a monk, nor admonish improper behavior in a monk, although monks retain the right to criticize nuns.[15]

In examining these rules, we must take into consideration the historical and cultural context that conditioned the formation of the Buddhist Sangha. The Bhikkhu Sangha had already been firmly established before the idea was raised of having a women's order. The acceptance of women into the Sangha required adjustments that were not always willingly accepted. In order to facilitate their acceptance into the Order, the Buddha needed to assure the bhikkhus that they had nothing to lose by the admission of women. The Bhikkhuni

Sangha had to meet expectations of Laity,
regardless of gender

Sangha was thus required to adopt the *Gurudharma* which placed them in a subordinant position to the bhikkhus.

But the Buddha intended the relationship between the two orders to be that of elder brothers to younger sisters, with all sharing the same essential status as children of the Buddha. Given the social climate of the time, the bhikkhunis' subordination to bhikkhus can be seen as a strategy to insure their protection in the Sangha. It was not intended that bhikkhunis were to be the bhikkhus' servants; when bhikkhus began to take advantage of their superior position and required the bhikkhunis to spend their time on chores and services rather than spiritual practice, the Buddha established rules forbidding this.[16] While the Buddha was alive, recurrent abuses of male privilege and power in the Sangha were kept in check.

The *Gurudharmas*, like all Buddhist teachings, were guidelines rather than rules cast in iron to be followed blindly. The first *Gurudharma* stated that bhikkhunis must always pay homage to bhikkhus, regardless of seniority. But when a group of monks behaved in an unseemly manner towards some bhikkhunis, the Buddha instructed the bhikkhunis not to pay respect to them, in effect "breaking" the first rule. Buddhist law is by nature flexible and responsive to the situation at hand; it is not static.

Although the eighth *Gurudharma* forbade bhikkhunis from commenting critically on the behavior of bhikkhus, Buddhist laywomen (and men) were allowed and even encouraged to do so. The relationship between the Sangha and laity was reciprocal: in exchange for material support, the Sangha was expected to provide spiritual guidance and exemplify the Buddhist teachings in their behavior. Therefore, even though the Bhikkhu Sangha was not answerable to the criticisms of female members of the Order, it was required to meet the expectations of the laity, regardless of gender.

According to the Buddhist texts, the *Gurudharmas* were given to Mahapajapati at the time of the formation of the Bhikkhuni Sangha. This has been accepted in Buddhist tradition until recently, as scholars have begun to question the historical origins of the *Gurudharmas*. Ven. Khantipalo, an English monk ordained in the Thai tradition, argues that since Mahapajapati herself was not required to undergo a two-year probation period prior to her ordination, as set down in the sixth rule, this rule may have been established later, after the Bhikkhuni Order had been in existence for some time. Khantipalo concluded that "the *Gurudharmas* have been backdated to Mahapajapati's ordination by some bhikkhus who were in charge of reciting the *Vinaya*."[17] The reason for their inclusion in the *Vinaya* was to emphasize the subordination of the bhikkhunis to the Bhikkhu Sangha.

Another frequently quoted statement from the texts has the Buddha proclaiming that by accepting women into the Sangha, the longevity of the Buddhist tradition will be shortened by 500 years. According to original predictions, this meant that Buddhism would last for 1,500 rather than 2,000 years. Whether the Buddha said it or not, the obvious untruth and negative gender bias of this statement has become clear. The tradition has now survived for over 2,500 years, moving from India into Southeast Asia, the Himalayan countries, the Far East, and now the West.

The development and longevity of both the Bhikkhu and Bhikkhuni Sanghas in India and Sri Lanka were closely related during the first millennium of the tradition. During King Asoka's reign in the third century B.C.E., Sanghamitta Theri and a group of learned bhikkhunis went to Sri Lanka and established a Bhikkhuni Sangha there, which was to last for more than a thousand years. In India proper, there is ample historical and archaeological evidence from inscriptions to establish the existence of a continuous Bhikkhuni Sangha until the tenth or eleventh century, when Indian Buddhism as a whole was eclipsed by the influx of Islam.

In Sri Lanka, Buddhism prospered with royal support. Both the *Mahavamsa* and *Dipavamsa*, chronicles that recount Sri Lanka's Buddhist history, mention the existence and activities of the Bhikkhuni Sangha. An inscription dating from the year 1057 describes a hospital run by bhikkhunis in Anuradhapura, the capital, illustrating active bhikkhuni involvement in social work.[18] In the eleventh century, political turmoil and the invasion of South India's Chola dynasty brought on the disappearance of the Buddhist Sangha in Sri Lanka. The Sri Lankan Bhikkhu Sangha was later revived by receiving the ordination lineage from Thailand, but the Bhikkhuni Sangha was less fortunate and was never revived in Sri Lanka.

The Sri Lankan bhikkhuni lineage, however, has survived in China. A group of Sri Lankan nuns were invited to help give ordination to a group of Chinese women in the year 433. This lineage is still active in China, and has been transplanted to Korea, Japan, and Vietnam.

Local Thai beliefs and customs reinforce the negative perception of women. Some of these attitudes are regarded by the population as coming from the Buddhist teaching and are believed to reflect Buddhist attitudes, and this has lent them greater credibility and increased influence. It is frequently said, for example, that "women were born from their bad karma." This assertion that being a woman is in itself negative does much damage to woman's self-image and creates obstacles to her spiritual and social development. According to Buddhist teaching, everyone is born according to his or her karma. The present situation of one's life is a direct reflection of one's actions, whether good or bad. The belief that one's gender is the result of "bad karma" does not hold any meaning. Yet many monks, whose principal source of support is laywomen, believe this idea. Many women are convinced that they carry a heavy load of negative karma due to the simple fact of their gender, and are therefore eager to gain merit to offset it. Making offerings to the Sangha is the primary way most laypeople hope to gain merit. Monks, being "fields of merit," thus benefit directly from this vicious belief.

A similarly negative belief that "women are of lower birth" reflects Brahmanical ideas of caste, rather than Buddhist teaching, which was remarkable in its rejection of the rigid social structure and social prejudices of sixth century B.C.E. India. The Buddha often explained that the quality of one's actions defined a person's worth, rather than birth into a particular social class or caste. Buddhist monks who hold what are in essence Brahmanical beliefs must be made aware that these were not the values of the Buddha, but are old prejudices based on ancient Indian cultural norms that were explicitly rejected by the Buddha.

Many Buddhist temples in Thailand, especially in the northern provinces, do not allow women to circumambulate the stupa or enter the main hall. Local monks justify this by explaining that sacred relics are usually placed in the center of the stupa at the time of

[handwritten top margin: vestiges of Brahmanic belief still found among Thai Sangha ⇒ "corruption" of Buddhism]

[handwritten left margin: author suggests a return to original texts in order to find 'authoritative solutions to such negative beliefs']

construction. If women were allowed to circumambulate the stupa, they would be walking above the sacred relics, which is considered disrespectful; and also that because women are "unclean" their presence would disempower the relics.

The concept that women are unclean stems from the physical fact of menstruation and ancient taboos against blood that are found in various cultures throughout the world. In Vedic India, the mystical power of mantras in sacred texts such as the *Arthavaveda* was believed compromised by proximity to blood. Sacred or ritually purified objects had to be protected from polluting influences. As it was awkward to know when women were menstruating, a general rule forbidding all women from coming into contact with sacred texts or objects was established.

During Thailand's Ayudhya period, Buddhist monks involved themselves with the study of the *Vedas*, often at the expense of Buddhist study. Many Brahmanical beliefs were absorbed into Thai religion and culture during this time. It is important to remember that such beliefs and practices, the vestiges of which are still found among the Buddhist Sangha in Thailand, are not Buddhist in origin and actually represent a corruption of Buddhism.

We have seen how some portions of the Buddhist texts and local beliefs have helped generate and maintain negative social values about women. Law and external social controls cannot completely counteract their effects, and it is necesary to go back to the texts themselves for authoritative solutions to such negative beliefs. Passages containing positive references to women can also be found in the texts, although these are as marked by the norms of ancient India as are the negative statements.

One of the primary difficulties in studying the Buddhist scriptures results from the fact that women (and laypeople) have long been denied access to these texts, primarily through lack of education. The texts are preserved in Pali, and the study of Pali was, and in many cases still is, the prerogative of an elite group of educated monks. In Thailand, the *Khom* script, known only to learned monks, was used in the translation of the Pali texts. A Thai translation of the *Tripitaka* has been available to the general public only since 1957. In addition, women have little opportunity to learn or study

[handwritten bottom margin: & denied access to B. scriptures ⇒ Lack of education —]

Buddhism, while most Thai men have a brief exposure to Buddhist education during their traditional three-month ordination in the rainy-season retreat. Whatever little Thai Buddhist laywomen and men know of the Buddhist texts comes to them in the form of Dharma talks from monks, subject to their selection and interpretation.

Today, education is more generally available to the public, and Buddhist texts are now available in both Thai and English. The forty-five volume edition of the original Pali Buddhist texts is now available in Thai in a condensed volume called *Tripitaka for the People*.[19] By consulting this, the reader can get a general picture of the scope of the texts before delving more deeply into a particular topic. Thai laymen and laywomen finally have the opportunity to read and study Buddhist writings.

The most positive passage regarding women in the texts was when the Buddha declared that men and women have equal spiritual potential. This acceptance and affirmation of human spiritual potential opened a new path for women in religious life. In contrast to the restrictions of Brahmanical society, a woman's spiritual development and salvation were no longer dependent on her social role in relationship to men, either husband or son.

Common religious and social values that gave preference to male offspring were challenged when King Pasenadi approached the Buddha in grief on hearing the news of the birth of a baby girl. The Buddha assured him that a "female child may prove even better than a boy," becoming virtuous, wise, reverent, respectful, a faithful wife, and mother of noble sons.[20] In a true Buddhist society, the birth of a boy or girl really makes no difference.

The Buddha recommended to his disciples to look upon every woman as if she were "your own mother or sister,"[21] and he taught laypeople that "to respect one's mother and one's wife is to be blessed."[22] While the texts speak of the "five woes" of women, they also relate their "five powers": form, wealth, relatives, sons, and morality. In the context of Indian society, these must be regarded as positive characteristics.

It is not surprising then that, given the context of Brahmanical social structure and values, the Buddha's positive attitude toward

33

women drew a great number of women to the Sangha. It was recorded in the texts that thousands of laywomen and bhikkhunis attained various levels of spiritual development. Among the bhikkhunis, at least thirteen were praised by the Buddha, including Mahapajapati, foremost in seniority; Patacara, foremost in *Vinaya*; and Dhammadinna, foremost in giving Dharma talks.[23] Many laywomen were also lauded for their spiritual qualities, including Visakha for *dana*, generosity and giving, Samavati for compassion, and Katiyani for unshakeable faith.

These successes of women, both lay and ordained, represented the completion of the four groups of Buddhists as instituted by the Buddha: monks, nuns, laymen, and laywomen. The growth or decline of Buddhism depends on the health and vitality of all four groups. Women should be given full support to bring forth their strength in Buddhism. They should be encouraged to become ordained if they so wish. The success of the bhikkhunis is compared in the texts to "the light of the Sangha."[24]

Concerned Buddhists must study closely the scriptures to glean from them the pure message of the Buddha, which is otherwise clouded by the imposition of cultural values and gender bias. Seemingly negative passages must be examined critically and not allowed to become barriers to the spiritual development of women. Conversely, positive passages should be brought to light to confirm and encourage women today. Buddhism cannot really blossom if half the world's population is not given its full right to express its religious commitment. Oppression within any religion reflects badly on those doing the oppressing and limits its effectiveness and vitality.

---

[1] *Anguttara Nikaya, Suttanta Pitaka,* Vol. XX, *Thai Tripitaka* (Bangkok: Department of Religious Affairs, 1957).

[2] Ven. Henepola Gunaratna, "Equality for Bhikkhuni[s]," in *NIBWA* no. 24, July-September 1990.

[3] Chatsumarn Kabilsingh, *A Comparative Study of the Bhikkhuni Patimokkha* (Varanasi: Chaukhamba Orientalia, 1984), pp. 32 *ff.*

[4] I.B. Horner, tr., *Books of the Discipline,* Vol. XX, *Sacred Books of the Buddhists* (London: Luzac & Co., 1963), p. 401.

[5] Boonsue Kornvibha, "Buddhism and Gender Bias: An Analysis of a *Jataka* Tale" (unpublished M.A. thesis, The Hague University, the Netherlands).

6 *Samyutta Nikaya*, Vol. I, *Thai Tripitaka*, p. 37.

7 Max Muller, ed., and T.W. Rhys Davids, trans., *Digha Nikaya, Buddhist Suttas* (Delhi: Motilal Banarsidass, 1965).

8 *Anguttara Nikaya*, Vol. I, *Thai Tripitaka*, p. 1.

9 *Samyutta Nikaya*, Vol. I, *Thai Tripitaka*, p. 85.

10 *Samyutta Nikaya*, Vol. XVIII, *Thai Tripitaka*, p. 297.

11 *Anguttara Nikaya*, Vol. II, *Thai Tripitaka*, p. 80.

12 Yuichi Kajiyama, "Women in Buddhism," *The Eastern Buddhist* (Kyoto, Autumn 1982).

13 "Bhikkhuni Sanghadisesa," no. 3. *Upato Patimokkha*. Pali version. (Bangkok, 1927).

14 "Bhikkhuni Pacittiya," no. 95. *Upato Patimokkha*. Pali version. (Bangkok, 1927).

15 Max Muller, ed., Vol. X, *Cullavamsa*, Vol. XX, *Sacred Books of the East* (Delhi: Motilal Banarsidass, 1965), p. 354.

16 Bhikkhu Nissagiya, "Pacittiya for Monks," nos. 4, 17, *Mahavibhanga, Vinaya Pitaka, Tripitaka for The People*. Sujeeb Buññanubarp, ed. (Bangkok: Terd Toon Tham Group, 1979), pp. 156, 159.

17 Ven. Khantipalo, "An Examination: On the Eight Serious Matters," in *NIBWA* no. 13, October-December 1987.

18 C. Mabel Rickmer, tr. *Cullavamsa* (Colombo: Ceylon Government Information Department, 1953), 46. 27.

19 Sujeeb Buññanubarp, ed., *Tripitaka for the People* (Bangkok: Terd Toon Tham Group, 1979).

20 C.A.F. Rhys Davids, tr., *Kindred Sayings, Samyutta Nikaya* (London: Luzac & Co., 1950), p. 111.

21 *Samyutta Nikaya*, Vol. IV, *Thai Tripitaka*, p. 110.

22 *Anguttara Nikaya*, Vol. III, *Thai Tripitaka*, p. 77.

23 *Anguttara Nikaya*, Vol. IV, *Thai Tripitaka*, p. 347.

24 *Anguttara Nikaya*, Vol. II, *Thai Tripitaka*, p. 8.

no Bhikkhuni Sangha
mae jis are w/o formal
ordination / lineage

Mae Jis

√ During seven hundred years of Buddhism in Thailand, there has never been an official Bhikkhuni Sangha. Thailand's situation contrasts with that of China, Sri Lanka, and other Buddhist countries where Bhikkhuni Sanghas were established to meet the need expressed by women to participate fully in religious life. However, there does exist a form of religious life for Thai Buddhist women, known as *mae ji.* Mae jis shave their heads, wear white robes, and observe either five or eight precepts while following a form of monastic life without formal ordination or proper ordination lineage.

The historical development of mae jis is difficult to trace. If they did exist in ancient times, all records of them were lost in the destruction of the capital at Ayudhya by the Burmese in the fifteenth century. The earliest extant record of them is found in the writings of S.D. La Loubère, a French missionary who traveled in Thailand in the late seventeenth century. He noted that most mae jis were old women living inside a few temple compounds where monks lived.[1] A German physician named Campfer, who visited Thailand around the same time, noted that the mae jis wore white, which distinguished them from the yellow-robed monks.[2] Without more historical evidence, it is impossible to know exactly how and when mae jis came into existence, but we do know that mae jis have existed in Thailand for at least three hundred years.

Women who led lives very much like mae jis existed during the Buddha's lifetime.[3] Known as *upasika* (laywomen) or *savika* (female followers), they wore white clothing and expressed their religious commitment by observing either eight or ten precepts. At the next level of commitment, women would shave their heads and join the Sangha either as *samaneris* (novices) or bhikkhunis.

The wearing of white was a prevalent practice in the diverse religious movements that flourished in sixth century B.C.E. India, such as the Ajivikas and the Jains. One of two Jain sects, the Svetambara, is called in the Thai language "white-cloth ji." The term "ji" may have been adopted from this source to describe the white-robed, shaven-headed mae jis. Some mae jis believe that "ji" is a shortened form of *jina,* meaning "one who has conquered," an epithet for the Buddha, or a spiritually advanced person. However, "jina" would more commonly be shortened to *jin* in Thai.

Other explanations give the source of the term in the phrase *ji dhatu,* "triumph," meaning one who is able to overcome negative mental influences;[4] from *laji,* meaning "shyness," a reference to female chastity;[5] or as a derivative of *pabbajita,* an ascetic or one who has been ordained.[6] Research from the Thai Department of Religious Affairs indicates that the connection between Thailand and Sri Lanka during the Ayudhya period may be the source of the term. Sri Lankan women who observed precepts and wore white were known as *upajivini,* literally, "better life." However, Sri Lankan upajivinis did not shave their heads, and the shortened version would more correctly be *jiv* (*jib* in Thai) rather than "ji."

There are many questions concerning the origin of the term "mae ji." In the Thai language, "ji" can refer to Buddhist monks, non-Buddhist groups such as Jains, and also to female Buddhists who observe precepts, have shaven heads, and wear white robes. With such a variety of usages, it is difficult to determine the actual etymology and literal meaning of the term as it relates to female Buddhists.

Besides mae jis, there are various other groups of Buddhist religious women in Thailand. They are distinguished by the number of precepts they undertake to observe, the color of their robes, and other criteria of behavior, length of time under the precepts, etc. *Silacarinis* wear brown robes, shave their heads, and observe ten precepts. A group of silacarinis began at Wat Chanasongkram in Bangkok in the 1960s. Since the death of the abbot who ordained them, their numbers have decreased. A few still practice meditation and observe the precepts, but their role is limited to within their own nunnery. Similar to the silacarinis, *sikhamats,* who also observe vegetarianism, received their ordination in the Bodhirak lineage. This group is trying to reintroduce a simple lifestyle and adhere closely to the form of early Buddhism. Due to involvement in politics, they were disestablished by the Thai government in 1989, although their case is still being debated in the courts. (These two

*mae jis seem to be
minimally legitimized
⇒ lack of legal status*

*they don't receive benefits
of sangha members
but are guided by
Restrictions*

THAI WOMEN IN BUDDHISM

groups are discussed in more detail in Chapter Six.)

A very small organization of women, called *buddha-savika*, wear yellow robes, shave their heads, and observe bodhisattva precepts. The chief nun of this sect received full bhikkhuni ordination in a Taiwanese lineage. (This group is discussed in more detail in Chapter Five.) Finally, *ji-praam* are women who undertake eight precepts for just a brief period of time, such as one week. For practical reasons, such as the fact that they will soon be returning to work, these women do not shave their heads.

The white-robed mae jis, however, constitute the majority of Thai religious women. Their number is disputed, but statistics from the Thai Department of Religious Affairs compiled for the years 1976-78 estimated that there were more than 10,000. According to a 1985 interview with Mae ji Arun, Secretary of the Institute of Thai Mae Jis, there are 5,000 mae jis officially registered with the Institute. Combined with unaffiliated mae jis throughout Thailand, the total number probably does not much exceed 10,000.

The existence of mae jis is not supported in the *Pali Canon* or by Thai law. Mae jis are regarded by Buddhist legalists to be upasikas; like mae jis, pious laywomen undertake to observe five or eight precepts. Despite the fact that mae jis shave their heads, wear white robes, and live a form of monastic life that distinguishes them from ordinary laywomen, they are not considered ordained persons, and thus are not under the jurisdiction of the Department of Religious Affairs. The Department's attitude toward mae jis is expressed by its annual report which includes detailed records on the monks, novices, and even temple boys in each temple, yet makes no mention of mae jis. An abbot is responsible for mae jis only on the basis that they are residents of the temple.[7] Their lack of legal status results in their being denied certain benefits enjoyed by monks, such as reduced fares on public transportation. Yet mae jis are also denied the right to vote in Thailand, as are official members of the Sangha, because they are supposed to have rejected worldly concerns.

catch 22

In the Buddhist community, the Sangha and the laity are interdependent. The Sangha provides spiritual guidance to the laity, and the laity, in turn, provides material support. The Buddha described the role of the Sangha towards laypeople: to "show their love for them, keep them from evil, encourage them to do good, feel for them with kindly thoughts, teach them what they have not heard before, correct and clarify what they have learned, and show them the way to heaven." The laypeople, in turn, should serve the Sangha with "kindly acts, words, and thoughts, by opening their homes to them and by supplying them with their material needs."[8]

As mae jis do not have an official legal position in the Sangha, the laity does not feel obligated to support them. In fact, to a great degree, Thai society holds the false view that the Buddha did not want women to join the Sangha. Monks, as fully ordained members of the Sangha, are seen as worthy "fields of merit" for offerings, but mae jis are not. To gain merit, people prefer to make offerings to monks rather than mae jis, even though monks already have adequate material support while mae jis struggle with meager resources. In addition, many Thai people do not think religious life is for women. Many feel that women who become mae jis do so because of some failure in their worldly lives, such as an unsatisfactory relationship or negligence on the part of their husbands or families.

Scattered all over the country without an overall organizational framework or clear set of responsibilities, there is a wide disparity in the behavior and degree of commitment to religious principles exhibited by mae jis. Some are women whose desire to join the mae ji community is a reflection of their denial of a world that has rejected them. Mae jis' lack of self-esteem, coupled with negative social attitudes, have resulted in their extremely low status. Marginalized, undereducated, and economically unsupported, mae jis are alienated in Thai society, garnering little support even from working women who feel that mae jis do not adequately represent their voice in Buddhism. At best, the majority of Thai people prefer to ignore them.

mae jis poor
self image

In 1969, the Sangharaja initiated a national meeting of mae jis, and the Institute of Thai Mae Jis was formed with his support. Its objectives were to unite mae jis from all over Thailand, work towards elevating and strengthening their status, help propagate Buddhism, contribute to social welfare, and help aged and destitute mae jis. A foundation was formed to support the Institute, and it was given legal status in 1972. The Institute has attempted to establish administrative structures for registering and organizing mae jis, but it has met with only partial success. However, the Institute has proved effective in screening and recommending potential candidates to nunneries and has also been active in various activities such as publishing books, providing practical and religious training and education for mae jis, and organizing social work.[9]

The Institute has also established a set of guidelines and regulations. A woman seeking to be a mae ji must know nine dharmas, which begin with asking for ordination, and include the observance of precepts. Many mae jis, however, do not know even these basic rules and are aware only that they are to observe the eight precepts and to behave in an appropriate manner. Mae jis have no formal ordination; a woman usually asks for the precepts from a monk or the head mae ji of the nunnery she intends to enter. Women who later wish to leave their life as a mae ji need only approach their original preceptors and ask for permission by reciting certain Pali verses.

The reasons women choose a religious life vary widely. Some women are motivated by a strong wish to develop themselves spiritually, while others seek release from the difficulties of their lives. This was true in the time of the Buddha, and it is true today.

According to recent research, Thai women who become mae jis do so for a combination of reasons. A majority, nearly three-quarters of the women surveyed, said that they became mae jis in order to study and practice Dharma. A full third also said that they were answering to vows, that is, fulfilling a promise if they recovered from an illness or overcame some other personal difficulty. About a quarter of those interviewed stated a wish to teach and help others, while only a small number stated their hope to attain *nirvana*, individual spiritual salvation, as a primary motivation.[10]

It is interesting to note the relatively low percentage (25%) of women whose primary concern in this role is working for social welfare. For some women, becoming a mae ji offers escape from worldly pressures and problems. For them, involvement in social work means a return to the world from which they are seeking release.

Most mae jis come from rural, low-income backgrounds, and therefore have received limited education. In rural Thailand, prejudicial preference of sons over daughters is especially evident in this regard; when financial resources for further education are available for only one child, it is always the boy who is given the chance. It is

mae jis are essentially servants of the sangha

also customary, as has been mentioned, for a young man to become a monk for three months when he comes of age, during which time he receives an elementary Buddhist education. Only 7% of mae jis have had ten years of formal education, 60% have had less than seven years, and many older mae jis are illiterate.[11] While a few mae jis have completed the highest levels of Pali study, and some serve as Pali teachers to monks and other mae jis, the number of such accomplished women is still too small to have much effect on mae jis' overall status. While monks have a choice of two Buddhist universities in Bangkok, mae jis do not have a place where they can receive a proper Buddhist education.

The lack of education severely limits the possibilities for mae jis in both the Sangha and society. Mae jis feel that, as part of the Sangha, they should be able to teach Dharma to laypeople and offer spiritual guidance. But in order to effectively fulfill this role, they themselves must be well versed in Buddhist texts and experienced in Dharma practice. Mae jis with only a primary education are often unable to offer a correct Buddhist understanding, falling back instead on superstitions and folk-beliefs, which limits their ability to teach. This is also true among poorly educated monks.

Mae jis living within temple compounds stay there with the permission of the abbot. In many temples, their standard of living is low and most are relegated to serving the temple by cooking and cleaning for the monks. Those who have some support from the abbot or the temple administration find survival as a mae ji barely possible. Those who do not have great difficulty making ends meet.

Many older mae jis have taken up begging in the belief that people would prefer giving money to them rather than ordinary beggars. Unfortunately, this has contributed to the poor public image of mae jis. Members of the Institute of Thai Mae Jis are particularly concerned about this practice and try to discourage it by placing older, destitute mae jis in old-age homes. But this does not address the root cause of the problem, which is the poverty of many mae jis due to the lack of institutional and societal support.

A few mae jis are fortunate enough to have private sources of support from relatives or friends. One mae ji from Petburi province, with financial assistance from her family, was able to start a nunnery on family-owned land. Despite the fact that she had only four years of formal education, she was able to create a successful, largely self-supporting nunnery. The mae jis there work in the fields growing seasonal crops, and go out on morning alms rounds as well. Another successful private nunnery, in Nakhonpathom province, is supported by the interest drawn on an endowment contributed by a wealthy woman benefactor. (Both these nunneries are discussed in greater detail in Chapter Five.)

Given the current state of affairs, mae jis are not in a strong position to organize themselves. They would like the Thai Department of Religious Affairs to establish legal procedures to ordain them. At a recent seminar on mae jis,[12] I suggested that they are also "fields of merit" worthy of dana, and that mae jis might help support each other. Several approached me afterwards to tell me that they were greatly encouraged by this proposal, which they had not previously considered possible. Nine monks were present along with nine mae jis at the opening ceremonies of Sakyadhita, the International Association of Buddhist Women, Thailand Chapter.[13] This set an example and helped to open up further possibilities for establishing mae jis as appropriate "fields of merit."

In the Buddha's time, there were many successful role models for women in the Sangha. However, through the long history of Buddhism in Thailand, these positive role models have been actively suppressed. Revival of the Bhikkhuni Sangha would be a very important way to elevate the status of women in religious life. Buddhist tradition maintains that there are five spiritual opportunities difficult to attain: being born as a human being, encountering a buddha, being able to "go forth," attaining confidence, and hearing the true teaching.[14] Preventing women from "going forth," from joining the Bhikkhuni Sangha, denies them the opportunity to express their spiritual lives to the fullest. Becoming a bhikkhu or bhikkhuni is important because it is the way to practice full-time, allowing the individual to deepen his or her understanding of the Buddha's teachings. It is also important to maintain the Sangha, which has been the vehicle for preserving the Buddhist teaching from the Buddha's lifetime to the present day.

There is great need for both Thai laywomen and mae jis to develop a path of Buddhist practice that integrates concern for social issues. The spirit of Buddhism is not escapism—one must be able to lead a religious life within a social context. In the modern world, there is an urgent need for the Buddhist community to understand the value of, and make available, a kind of Buddhist practice that can be applied on an everyday basis.

Based on the study of the problems and difficulties faced by mae jis, the following suggestions attempt to answer their unmet needs. Most important is the establishment of an ordination procedure. The Thai Department of Religious Affairs must review this issue with new insight and greater understanding. It must seriously consider the problems faced by mae jis, and reassess its position that, as they are not ordained, they are not the responsibility of the Department. The existence of mae jis reflects a real need felt by Thai Buddhist women to lead committed religious lives, and the Department should consider its responsibility to provide more opportunities for women to join spiritual communitites. For administrative streamlining, nunneries should be set up at a few designated temples, instead of being scattered throughout the country as they now are. Head mae jis can help lessen the monks' administrative burden by taking on the responsibility of supervising and reporting to the regional committee on the mae jis in their charge. Women who wish to take the robe for a short period of time should remain ji-praam with unshaven heads, to distinguish them from more permanent mae jis. The term "mae jis" might be replaced by a more appropriate one, such as *savika* (Skt: *sravaka*), a female follower of the Buddha.

To help increase educational opportunities for mae jis, a central organization is needed, with help from both the government and non-governmental organizations. Long-term educational planning should begin at the seventh grade level and include both general and Buddhist education. Future planning for college-level education is also necessary, to equip mae jis with the training needed to function effectively as spiritual counselors to many different kinds of people. There is also a great need to train mae jis for leadership. For some mae jis, leadership qualities may emerge naturally with better education, but training in how to apply these qualities is still necessary. In the immediate future, mae jis need to be brought together to create a forum for discussing the problems they face. Mae jis need a kind of basic training in the precepts and the other rules they are required to follow and an understanding of what Thai society expects of

mae jis need positive attitude from Sangha!

them. This will give them self-confidence and a positive approach to the world, as well as a solid foundation in Buddhist principles for their spiritual development.

Finally, a positive attitude from the Sangha is of vital importance. In the past, the monks have not played a role in supporting mae jis. In order for Buddhism to be firmly grounded and to grow and develop, we need both men and women to be rooted in the Buddhist teaching. Monks are limited by the *Vinaya* from having close contact with women. It is therefore necessary for mae jis to carry on the work of sharing the Dharma with women. In order to be effective, mae jis need, at the very least, the moral support of the monks. The attitude of the monks towards mae jis must develop with their understanding of the crucial role mae jis can fill in Thai Buddhism. The position of the monks in the Sangha is not threatened, and by joining in the effort to make available the Buddha's teaching to all members of society, Buddhism and society as a whole will benefit.

mae jis do not threaten position of monks in Sangha

[1] S.D. La Loubère, *The Kingdom of Siam* (Oxford: Oxford University Press, 1986), part 3, p. 113.

[2] *Mae Ji Sarn*, no. 9, May-July 1971, p. 29.

[3] Ven. Prakru Nidesdharmakarn, *Mae ji's Life* (Bangkok, 1981), pp. 23-25.

[4] *The Handbook of Mae Jis' Regulations* (Bangkok, 1978), p. 71.

[5] Rearn Attavibulya, "Ji, Yai Ji," *Thai Culture* (Bangkok: No. 17, October 1978), p. 41.

[6] *Jis' Ordination and Rules of Persons Practicing Vipassana Karmathan* (Bangkok: Bangkok Press, 1980), p. 1.

[7] *Monks' Constitution* (Bangkok: Department of Religious Affairs, 1962), p. 37.

[8] T.W. Rhys Davids, ed., *Sigalovada Suttanta*, Vol. IV, *Sacred Books of the Buddhists* (London: Pali Text Society, 1965), p. 183.

[9] Prakhong Singhanartnitirak, "Role of Thai Mae Jis in Social Development" (unpublished M.A. thesis, Thammasat University, Bangkok, 1973), pp. 13-15.

[10] Quoted by Parichart Suwanbuppa in "The Roles of Christian Nuns and Buddhist Nuns" (unpublished M.A. thesis, Mahidol University, 1987), pp. 187-8.

[11] Working Committee for Long Range Plan in Women's Development, Report to the National Women's Council, 1981.

[12] Held at Wat Umong, Chiengmai, on June 9, 1989.

[13] Held at Watra Songdharma Kalyani, Nakhonpathom, on October 14, 1989 .

[14] Saya U Chat Tin, *Maha Bodhi Journal*, Vol. 95, nos. 4-6, p. 41 *ff*.

CHAPTER FIVE

Two Bhikkhuni Movements in Thailand

Although, as we have seen, there has never been an official Bhikkhuni Sangha in Thailand, a few women have attempted to become bhikkhunis. In 1928, two young sisters, Sara and Chongdi Bhasit, with their father's encouragement, received the samaneri ordination. At the time, Sara, the elder sister, was eighteen years old. Their father, Pra Panom Saranarin (Khlueng Bhasit), felt strongly that bhikkhunis needed to be represented in the Thai Sangha. He hoped that bhikkhuni ordination would provide a meaningful way of religious life for women and also help to improve their social status.

During an interview with Sara, who is now eighty-one years old, she did not want to disclose the name of the master who gave her ordination for fear that he might encounter difficulty in remaining in the Sangha. At the time of their ordination, the Ven. Bhikkhu Ard of Wat Khaoyoi in Petburi province was suspected of having given ordination to these two women and was forced, as a consequence, to leave the Sangha.

The two sisters remained samaneris and received bhikkhuni ordination in 1932. Apparently Sara and Chongdi received their vows only from monks. According to the ordination rules, proper bhikkhuni ordination requires that the preceptor giving ordination be a senior monk of at least ten years' standing, recognized and appointed as such by the Sangha. A minimum of five monks must attend the ordination, and the applicant must first receive ordination from the Bhikkhuni Sangha before receiving it from the Bhikkhu Sangha. As there is no official Thai Bhikkhuni Sangha in existence, the Thai Sangha did not consider Sara and Chongdi to have been properly ordained.

At the time in question, both sisters stayed at Wat Nariwong (literally, "female lineage") which had been built on land given them by their father in his own compound. Pra Panom Saranarin had offered the land to the Sangha but had been refused, as they considered him someone who was going against Buddhist tradition. The temple was used as a center for Dharma discussion for local people interested in Buddhist teaching and practice.

During their residence at Wat Nariwong, located on the bank of the Chao Praya River, the two bhikkhunis sometimes went for alms in the neighboring community. Although some people spoke harshly of them, others offered them food. They also traveled to different temples where they were given shelter with the mae jis, and they went on alms rounds, just like the monks.

During their travels, Sara and Chongdi stayed at Wat Pra Buddhapat in Saraburi province. It was local custom for laypeople to put only cooked rice in the bowl, placing other dishes on a tray held by the temple boy who followed the monks on alms rounds. The bhikkhunis had no temple boy to follow them, and for the first three days they received only cooked rice. When the local people realized this, they assured them that food would be brought for them to the temple. Other mae jis joined them, and together they formed a group of eight bhikkhunis.

Pra Panom Saranarin was a controversial figure politically, who was involved in many publications, such as *Naew Na* ("Front Lines"), *Nam Thai* ("Leading Thai"), and *Saradharma* ("Essence of the Dharma"). The titles of these publications reflect his progessive thinking. Most of his writings challenged the Thai government and raised issues about social injustice prevalent in the Thai society of his day. He was especially vocal about the decline of the Sangha leadership. His printing press was closed down by the government many times. Pra Panom Saranarin's public criticism of both the government and the Sangha placed him in a highly undesirable position. Subsequently, his daughters and the Bhikkhuni Sangha that he supported became targets of political wrath.

The Sangha was opposed to both the samaneri and the bhikkhuni ordinations. The Sangharaja sent a personal letter to the mayor of Nonthaburi, the province where their home temple was situated, ordering the bhikkhunis to disrobe and declaring the ordination invalid. In addition, the monks were informed that ordaining women as sikhamanas, samaneris, and bhikkhunis was not allowed.[1] Two monks, Pra Sasanasobhon of Wat Makut and Somdej Pra

Buddhakosacaraya of Wat Sudat, stated that ordaining women was the act of a crazy person, and they reiterated the traditional view that women were the enemy of monks' purity.

There was a violent reaction in the public media as well. Newspapers generally ridiculed the ordination of women. *Thai Num* ("Young Thai Men") considered such ordination the enemy of Buddhism and an act of Devadatta's followers.[2] *Lak Muang* ("City Post") considered the women's ordination a heretical act, deserving the death sentence. *Sri Krung* encouraged the government to punish these women. *Bangkok Karnmueng* ("Bangkok and Politics") suggested that if Pra Panom Saranarin was a good Buddhist, he should not allow his daughters to become heretics. Only one newspaper, *Ying Thai* ("Thai Women"), gave a positive report on the ordination of women.

Finally, police arrested the young bhikkhunis, and they were forced to appear in court at Nonthaburi. Some elderly bhikkhunis disrobed before the policemen arrived at the temple, but Sara and Chongdi refused to give up their robes. They were charged with an act of disobedience to the Order of the Sangha. Sara was jailed for eight days, Chongdi for four. At their father's suggestion, they started wearing brown robes similar to those of Japanese monks when they were released, but as soon as police harassment stopped, they resumed wearing their yellow robes.

After their arrest, the two bhikkhunis continued to travel to different provinces. Some temples offered them shelter, while others refused to admit them out of fear of reprisal from the authorities. At Kongchak ("Dharma Wheel") temple in Supanburi province, the abbot, Ven. Bhikkhu Kot, allowed the two bhikkhunis and two other samaneris to stay in his temple, against the wishes of senior administrative monks. The abbot explained that as it was customary for the temple to give shelter to any monks, even foreign monks, who followed good practice, he saw no reason against doing so for these well-behaved bhikkhunis. He told them that if they did not think it was right, they should inform the bhikkhunis of their objections personally.

Sara remained in robe as a bhikkhuni for two years before disrobing in the face of unrelenting pressure from society and from the

Buddhist authorities. In total, she remained an ordained person for eight years—a mae ji for two years, a samaneri for four, and a bhikkhuni for two years. Interviewed in 1983, when she was seventy-three years old, Sara's hair was cotton white but she was physically and mentally able. Despite the pressures and difficulties she had encountered in her quest to become a bhikkhuni, she still felt strongly about establishing a Bhikkhuni Sangha in Thailand, stating, "We should mend whatever is incomplete—a chair with a broken leg must be fixed. The Buddha established four groups of Buddhists: bhikkhus, bhikkhunis, laymen, and laywomen. As the Bhikkhuni Sangha is now missing, we have to reestablish this for the sake of completion."

She went on to say, "We do not have any bhikkhunis in Thailand because Buddhism originated in India. It was neither convenient nor safe for women to travel, so the Bhikkhuni Sangha never traveled to Thailand. During King Asoka's period, the king asked an arahat monk how he could become a relative of the *Sasana* (Buddhism). The monk replied that one could become a relative of the Sasana by ordaining one's son or daughter. So King Asoka allowed his daughter, Princess Sanghamitta, to be ordained as a bhikkhuni. The Buddha said that wherever there is Dharma, there is the way. So I think when there are people practicing Dharma, we should also have bhikkhunis."

However, following the strong conflict that Sara, Chongdi, and their father, Pra Panom Saranarin, experienced with the Sangha and the authorities, attempts to establish the ordination of women ceased.

As is clearly illustrated from Sara and Chongdi's story, Thai society is, in general, negatively disposed towards the idea of reviving the Bhikkhuni Sangha. No further attempt to bring about bhikkhuni ordination occurred until 1956, when Mrs. Voramai Kabilsingh, having received eight precepts from Pra Pronmuni of Wat Bovornnives, started to wear a light yellow robe to distinguish herself from the local white-robed mae jis. She also referred to herself as *nak-buad* (an ordained person).

Voramai Kabilsingh was born in 1908 in Rajburi province in central Thailand, and received part of her early education at a Catholic convent. As a schoolteacher she enrolled in a physical training course and became the first Thai woman to train in jujitsu (judo), boxing, and swordfighting. In 1932, at the age of twenty-four, Voramai joined a group of Boy Scouts on a twenty-eight day bicycle journey to Singapore, becoming the first Thai woman to make such a journey. She later explained that she wanted to show her students that gender difference does not prevent women from achieving such physical feats.

During the Second World War, she married Mr. Kokiat Shatsena, a member of parliament for Trang, a southern province. While he sat in the parliament as an MP, she was also there working as a news reporter. This work exposed Voramai to many social problems, and the lack of education for poor, rural children became a particular concern. As her husband became more deeply involved in politics, she became more interested in religion. They took their separate paths without legal separation, with one child from the marriage, and three adopted children.

During 1953, her interest in Buddhist meditation practice deepened, and in 1955 she began publishing a monthly Buddhist magazine, which was to last for more than thirty-two years. The magazine was a forum for a variety of articles on the teachings of Buddhism, and also on the role of women in Buddhism.

Voramai's work and her interest in Buddhism continued to intensify, and on May 2, 1956, she shaved her head and asked for eight precepts from Pra Pronmuni, Vice Abbot of Wat Bovornnives. This senior monk sat on the national Council of Elders and had also been one of the two teachers when the present king of Thailand, Bhumipol, received his ordination. He enjoyed a position of respect and authority in the council and was known for his strictness. Voramai wore a white robe at the time of her ordination but informed her preceptor that she would be adopting a light yellow robe to distinguish herself from the local mae jis. This was done intentionally, to protect her preceptor from incurring any blame should trouble arise.

Voramai followed a strict vegetarian diet (most Thai monks and lay Buddhists are not vegetarian), explaining that one cannot possibly generate compassion with sincerity of heart for all beings while still eating the flesh of animals. Within the same year that she took the precepts, a few young women joined her in becoming yellow-robed nuns. She was particular about training them in proper demeanor. When they traveled, they always walked in line according to seniority, and they were not allowed to travel alone, always going in pairs or larger groups. This small group of nuns received Dharma training and also learned handicrafts.

In 1957, Voramai purchased property in Nakhonpathom province, west of Bangkok, for the purpose of constructing a temple. Completed in a few years, Watra Songdharma Kalyani was the first temple in Thailand established by and for Buddhist women. At the same time, Voramai opened a private school for children from kindergarten to grade six, which also functioned as an orphanage. In one particular year, there were eighty nuns and orphans registered in her temple. There was also a printing press to handle the publication of a monthly magazine. To support themselves, the nuns worked both in the school and the printing press.

From 1960 to 1980, Voramai expanded her activities to include providing food, clothing, and medicine for the poor and needy. The first week that refugees from Cambodia crossed the border into Thailand, Voramai and her followers were there to give them 400 boxes of clothing. Today, in her eighties, she still engages in social welfare work by donating books and writing materials to neglected schools in isolated rural villages.

Voramai's service is not limited to laypeople, but also embraces the Sangha. She led her followers in providing robes and the "eight requisites" so that more than a hundred poor village men could receive ordination. She has donated Buddha images to temples and Buddhist centers in bordering provinces where there was a need for them.

Because the majority of her disciples are working people who come to the temple only on weekends, Voramai holds a regular service every Sunday, in which she gives a Dharma talk, leads meditation practice, and makes offerings, dedicating the merit to all sentient beings. Everyone who comes to the temple on Sunday shares in a vegetarian lunch. Teachers from other Buddhist traditions are also invited to give Dharma talks at Watra Songdharma

victory!

Kalyani, such as the Ven. Sopa of the Tibetan tradition from the United States, Dagpo Rinpoche of the Tibetan tradition from France, and others.

Not long after she established the temple, the mayor of Nakhonpathom province became suspicious of Voramai's activities and tried to link them to those of her politician husband, who belonged to the opposition party. The mayor reported her to the Council of Elders, charging that her activities were opposing the authority of the Sangha. The strongest objections were to her wearing yellow robes and naming the temple "Watra," reminiscent of "wat," the term used for a temple belonging to monks.

Voramai was summoned, interrogated, and threatened by the sheriff to change her robe, but she refused. Her case was sent to the Department of Religious Affairs in the late 1950s, and was subsequently presented to the Council of Elders. Her precepter, Pra Pronmuni, a respected member of the Council, quietly told the committee that he had given her ordination and simply asked the committee members, "Can we wear this color (light yellow)?" The committee members replied in the negative. He then stated that if monks cannot wear light yellow robes, the council should have no objection to Voramai's wearing them.

As to the second objection, it was decided that since the word "watra" simply means "practice," the name of the temple "Watra Songdharma Kalyani" means "a place where women perform Dharma practice," and there could be no objection to such usage. The council's brief verdict stated: "She has done nothing to defy the Sangha."

This was the only time Voramai experienced open conflict with the government. While waiting for her case to be heard, she fought in a quiet way. She had a piece of white cloth placed over the word "watra" in front of her temple, and made a public appeal in her monthly magazine, asking for any lawyer to come forward who could give her a reasonable explanation of the wrongdoing of which she was accused. Lawyers who responded could not find any breach of law. When Voramai was fully ordained as a bhikkhuni in a Chinese lineage, the Theravada Sangha in Thailand refused to legally verify her ordination. She therefore remains a Mahayana bhikkhuni. At best, the Thai government does not interfere with her.

Voramai has always been puzzled by the position of Thai nuns under Buddhism. She read of and was much inspired by bhikkhunis of the Buddha's time. But all the Thai monks whom she asked about this issue responded in the same manner—that there can be no bhikkhuni ordination since this requires dual ordination from both the bhikkhu and bhikkhuni sanghas. Since there has never been a Bhikkhuni Sangha in Thailand, such ordination is not possible.

However, Voramai believed that as the Bhikkhuni Sangha was established by the Buddha, any Buddhist woman who wanted to become ordained should be regarded as a bhikkhuni. In 1960, she went to Bodh Gaya, India, and requested direct ordination from the Buddha under the Bodhi tree, where the Buddha had become enlightened. She then spent two weeks in meditation there.

In 1971, she learned about the possibility of receiving ordination from the Chinese Bhikkhuni Sangha, who had received their lineage from Sri Lanka. She traveled to Taiwan and requested special ordination. Unaware that ordination is usually given annually in Hong Kong and Taiwan, Voramai had to wait for three weeks. The Ven. Bhikkhu Ming San, a monk from mainland China who was in Taiwan at the time, took the trouble of getting permission and sending invitations to various masters to participate in this special ordination. The Ven. Master Tao An, a well-known scholar and editor of the Buddhist magazine *The Lion's Roar*, agreed to serve as master and preceptor, along with twelve others. The Ven. Voramai Kabilsingh was ordained at Sung San Temple in Taipei. Her ordained name is Ta Tao ("The Great Way"), but on her return to Thailand she continues to be known by her former name. She is the first Thai woman to have received full ordination as a bhikkhuni in the Dharmagupta sub-sect of the Theravada tradition.[3]

To the general public in Thailand, Voramai is still only a mae ji. To the Thai Sangha, her status is at best that of a Mahayana bhikkhuni, and she is not considered to be part of the Thai Theravadin tradition. The Thai Sangha believes that the Theravada order of bhikkhunis is extinct and cannot be revived from Chinese Mahayana tradition.

Historically, however, it has been established that Chinese women received their lineage from Sri Lankan bhikkhunis in the Theravadin tradition. Moreover, the monastic rules followed by the

Chinese Sangha is that of the Dharmagupta, a sub-sect of Theravada Buddhism. This clearly establishes that the Chinese ordination lineage is Theravadin, although this fact is unknown to most Theravadin monks. Those who do know of it prefer not to acknowledge it. Recently, increasing numbers of women are receiving ordination in the West, particularly in the United States, along with women from Sri Lanka and Nepal. It is time for our Buddhist sisters to claim their rightful heritage as given by the Buddha. The position of Buddhist nuns is a reflection of the health of the Buddhist community as a whole, and a vital Bhikkhuni Sangha is essential to the continued development of the Buddhist community.

While these two bhikkhuni movements span a period of some thirty years, the women involved are contemporaries. Sara and her sister Chongdi's desire to become bhikkhunis met with heated opposition especially from the media and the Sangha, a reflection of the extreme conservatism of the time, nearly thirty years before Voramai's ordination. While Sara was forced by unrelenting societal pressure to disrobe, Voramai has been able to wear the robe for the last thirty-four years. Voramai's relative success owes much to change in Thai society, as well as her ability to negotiate with the authorities and avoid unnecessary conflict. She also enjoys the benefits of a solid educational and social background that has provided her with a strong foundation and prepared her for constructively negotiating through the difficulties in opening up the spiritual path for women.

Both women bravely expressed their rights concerning their spiritual needs. The Thai bhikkhus have enjoyed the monopoly of the Sangha for more than seven hundred years, from the time Thailand first formed itself into a kingdom. The adjustment needed to make a place for the Bhikkhuni Sangha may seem difficult, but it is not impossible. If the Bhikkhu Sangha truly understands the spirit of Buddhism, it must realize that the spiritual path is open to both men and women equally. Women have been strong supporters of the Sangha throughout its history. Any religious institution holding a bias against women undermines its claim to be a religion of enlightenment, since enlightenment is impartial as to gender, race, or any other distinction.

Buddhists in general must be mature in their understanding of the teaching of Buddhism in order to lend meaningful support to the

Sangha. Women who wish to lead lives as bhikkhunis are relatively few in number. This way of life is not easy or comfortable, but it provides an opportunity for such women to help themselves and others. The fear that too many women will leave the household life is without basis. While the decision to walk this path is entirely up to the individual, it is vitally important that the Buddhist institution provide the opportunity for those who wish to do so. Rather than obstructing them, the Bhikkhu Sangha should open the way for women to attain the spiritual heritage granted them by the Buddha.

---

[1] *Satridasana*, Vol. 1, No. 4, November 1983-January 1984.

[2] Devadatta was the Buddha's cousin who tried to bring about a schism in the Sangha.

[3] There were eighteen schools reported at the time of King Asoka, twelve belonging to the Theravada tradition, and six to the Mahasanghika. Dharmagupta is one of the twelve schools of Theravada.

CHAPTER SIX

Important Nun's Communities

Generally, there are two main types of residence for Buddhist nuns, either in a separate community within the administrative structure of formal wats, or in separate nunneries. In the latter case, nuns may receive Dharma instruction from a certain wat but generally are very much on their own. Separate, independent nunneries are gaining popularity among progressive mae jis.

The Institute of Thai Mae Jis, founded in the 1960s with the purpose of uniting and organizing mae jis throughout the country, has a small office at Mahamakut Buddhist University in Wat Bovornnives, and has more than eleven branches in Bangkok and throughout Thailand. Functioning primarily as an umbrella organization to oversee and regulate mae jis, the institute serves as the administrative parent for all branches and helps establish administrative procedures for newly formed nunneries. The institute also organizes Pali and Dharma classes in the nunneries and produces a quarterly magazine, *Mae Ji Sarn*, on the activities of mae jis, among other activities and services. One of its most important functions is to establish guidelines and monitor the activities of its members, in order to reduce the number of those who create a bad image for mae jis and the institute. This is especially important in raising public esteem and support for mae jis.

Members of the institute also engage in social work, such as establishing youth centers, providing teachers for Buddhist Sunday schools and kindergarten classes, offering day-care for preschool children, helping in the refugee camps on Thailand's eastern border, offering assistance to victims of natural disasters, and other activities.

The Institute of Thai Mae Jis Foundation, established in 1962 under the royal patronage of H.M. the Queen, is run by a nine-member committee. It provides support for the activities of the Institute of Thai Mae Jis, and helps fund educational programs for mae jis, both in Pali and Buddhist teaching and in practical skills. The

Foundation also engages in public relations work for the Institute, and social welfare programs.[1]

A good example of a branch nunnery of the Institute of Thai Mae Jis is Paktho in Rajburi province. There are sixty mae jis, and twenty-one young girls from thirteen to seventeen years old, who also observe eight precepts like the mae jis. Paktho is headed by Mae ji Prathin Kwan-on, age forty-six, who holds a master's degree from an Indian university.[2]

In 1990, this nunnery started a school called "Dhammacarini" for mae jis and young girls, beginning at the secondary school level teaching both general education and Buddhism. It is hoped that the "Dhammacarini" program will help to provide mae jis and other young women a solid educational foundation to prepare them for future involvement in social development work.

The members of Paktho Nunnery work at simple agriculture, growing different kinds of vegetables for their own use. In addition, twenty-one mae jis go out for daily alms rounds in the neighboring villages, and the alms food is shared by everyone in the nunnery during communal meals. Besides regular classes, both the mae jis and the girls participate in morning and evening chanting and meditation. Over time, Paktho might turn out to be a model to be followed by other nunneries. However, financial assistance is still very much needed. Part of the nunnery's regular financial support comes from a senior monk in Bangkok who understands the need to improve the education of mae jis and young girls.

Bunthawee Nunnery, popularly known as Thamglaeb, is situated in the Muang district, Petburi province. There are more than 100 mae jis, age thirty and older, who are financially self-supporting and provide their own meals. Few go out on alms rounds. One of the oldest nunneries, Bunthawee tends to serve mostly elderly women seeking a quiet life.

Thirty mae jis live in quarters within Wat Cha-am in Prajuab-khirikhan province. Although not a separate nunnery, the mae jis take care of their own separate meals. They attend morning and evening chanting and Dharma study classes.

Wat Chana Songgram is situated in Bangkok's Bangklampoo district, with thirty to forty mae jis, most of whom are young to middle-aged. The mae jis attend Dharma and Pali classes. Some of them receive regular support from their families or friends, while others are supported by the temple. Among the women who have trained at this temple is Mae ji Somsi Charuping, who has completed the highest level of achievement in Pali study. She is now working as a translator for the Bhumipalo Foundation at Wat Sraket in Bangkok.

Wat Chao-moon is situated on Jarunsanitwong Road, Tha-pra, Thonburi, on the western side of Chao Praya River. There are twenty to thirty mae jis of all ages. They follow the usual routine of a traditional nunnery, including morning and evening chanting and meditation periods. Here, mae jis have to provide their own financial support, either through private donations or help from their families. Very few depend on the temple for support.

Wat Pa Dhamma-Sobhon is in the Muang district, Lopburi province. "Wat Pa" means "forest temple." There are approximately seventy mae jis, ranging in age from twenty to seventy. There is a main kitchen where the mae jis can have communal meals, although some prefer to prepare meals separately. There are large Dharma, Pali, and *Abhidharma* classes.

Wat Kampaenglaeng is situated in the Muang district, Petburi province, with approximately thirty mae jis who support themselves on an individual basis, each one taking care of her own meals. There is a Dharma study class.

Wat Mahathat on Maharaj Road, Tha-prachan, Bangkok, was the royal temple of King Rama I and was closely associated with the palace of the Prince of the Front, now the campus of Thammasat University. There is no separate nunnery; approximately forty mae jis live in a separate area of the temple, the majority of whom are elderly. Some of them have to cook for themselves and some depend on the temple for their meals. Wat Mahathat is a major temple with an educational center for Dharma, Pali, and *Abhidharma* classes. Mae jis have an opportunity to attend some of these classes, but they are not allowed to attend Maha Chula Buddhist University, also in the same compound. Besides their religious practices, many mae jis are responsible for fundraising activities, including selling incense and flowers.

Nekkham Nunnery is another branch of the Institute of Thai Mae Jis, situated in the Muang district, Petburi province. There are approximately twenty mae jis, ages ranging from twenty to sixty. Mae jis here go out on alms rounds, but not on a regular basis. They also receive support from their families and from donations. There are Dharma study classes for the mae jis.

Wat Paknam, Pasicharoen district, Thonburi, has approximately two to three hundred mae jis, the largest concentration of mae jis in Thailand. Pra Mongkonthepmuni (Sod), the late abbot of Wat Paknam, was well-known throughout the country for his ability to heal through meditation, with a meditation technique that is very similar to the Tibetan visualization techniques. Among his disciples were many mae jis, who were noted for their obedience, great faith, and endurance. Many of these became his successors in this art of healing.[3] This respected role, recognized from the time of the former abbot, helped gain recognition for mae jis, and explains the unusually large mae ji community at Wat Paknam.

Mae jis here range from age twelve to eighty and come from various economic backgrounds. In the main kitchen, mae jis take turns helping with cooking for the monks, the other mae jis, and laypeople. It is understood that if they do not participate in the communal meals, they will be responsible for preparing separate meals for themselves. Mae jis in this nunnery are involved in many activities such as the Mae Ji Volunteers Project and Dharma Land-Golden Land, a project organized by the National Women's Council, as well as taking care of kitchen work, cleaning and maintaining the temple compound, taking care of the temple income and accounts, and attending Dharma and Pali classes organized and taught by mae jis. There are also meditation courses, including meditation for healing. A great number of laypeople attend meditation practice courses on a regular basis.

A body of academic research and writing on mae jis has resulted from the observation and study of mae jis at Wat Paknam. Scholars or others with a particular interest in contemporary Buddhist nuns in Thailand usually come here to get firsthand information. Mae jis in this temple are considered better-off than most, and the picture of mae jis one gets from this temple is not generally representative of the rest of Thailand or even of Bangkok.

The founder of Prachumnari Nunnery was King Rama V's consort; therefore, it is also known as "Samnak Chao Chom," "Chao Chom" being a title for the king's consort. It is situated in the precincts of Wat Mahathat, in the Muang district, Rajburi province. There are as many as one hundred mae jis between the ages of twenty and eighty. Each one provides her own meals, and there are Dharma and Pali classes.

Ratnapaiboon Nunnery is situated in Soi Maiyalarb, Bangkaen, Bangkok. Mae ji Arun Pet-urai, the secretary general of the Institute of Thai Mae Jis, is the chief nun of this small nunnery. Mae jis here support themselves from morning alms rounds through private donations. They provide a meditation center and Dharma classes as well as engage in the production of handicrafts.

Sanaam Ji Nunnery is in a secluded area reserved for mae jis in Wat Sanaam Praam, in the Muang district, Petburi province. There are more than one hundred women, ranging in age from twenty-two to eighty. Most of them are self supporting, and take their meals separately. The nunnery has a foundation which provides a small stipend for some mae jis, granted according to seniority. Mae jis at Sanaam Ji follow the normal routine of morning and evening chanting and meditation, and attend Dharma classes. The mae jis also make offerings of food to the monks in the same temple.

Sanaam Ji is considered one of the larger nunneries. From my observation, mae jis here live together, but do not really form a community together. Their separate financial support is partly responsible for a sense of aloofness. Outside of their routine activities, they are not organized to work towards common goals. This criticism can also be applied to many of the major nunneries in Thailand.

Santisuk nunnery, in Tha-tamnak, Nakhonchaisi district, Nakhonpathom province, was originally on a compound in Bangkok donated by a devoted Buddhist laywoman. Later, the compound proved to be too small, so the nunnery moved to its present location. The original benefactor also left some funds to support the nunnery under the supervision of the Mahamakut Foundation which is presided over by the present Sangharaja. In addition to covering construction costs, the nunnery receives monthly support from the foundation. Each mae ji receives a monthly stipend according to her seniority in the community.

In 1986, there were fifty mae jis, ages ranging from the late teens to the seventies. Among them were two Nepali nuns who came to study Buddhism in Thailand. The daily routine here is similar to other nunneries, including morning and evening chanting and group meditation sessions. Some mae jis are progressing in Dharma study, but they must go to other temples where advanced study is available.

The mae jis prepare their meals separately, depending on each one's financial capacity. Although they live in the same place, there is little sense of community living. However, mae jis here are known for their comparatively strict discipline and have established a good reputation.

Wat Siripong-Dhamnimit is in the Bangkapi district of Bangkok. There are approximately fifty mae jis, mostly older women. They follow the usual religious routine and take their meals at the temple.

Situated within Wat Soi Thong in Bangsue, Bangkok, is a nunnery of approximately fifty mae jis of all ages. Each one provides for her own meals separately. The mae jis, receiving no support from the temple, rely on private, family support. They follow the usual routine of morning and evening chanting and meditation.

NUNNERIES WITH UNIQUE CHARACTERISTICS

The nuns discussed in this category are a small minority, but they represent alternative approaches to religious life for Buddhist women in Thailand. In each example, the women have established different practices which they have found meaningful to their spiritual development. Some of them still wear white robes in accordance with traditional mae jis, but their activities and lifestyle are different. Some wear brown or yellow robes.

Watra Songdharma Kalyani, discussed in detail in Chapter Five, is the only example of a nunnery which uses the term "watra" in its name, emphasizing its function as a place of practice for Buddhist women. The temple was built in 1957 and claims to be first temple for Buddhist women in Thailand. The founder and abbess, Bhikkhuni Ta Tao (Voramai Kabilsingh), was the first Thai woman to receive full ordination from Taiwan and establish herself in Thailand. She wears the yellow robe of the Chinese tradition.[4]

The temple holds a regular Sunday service which includes a

Dharma talk by Bhikkuni Ta Tao, or other guest Buddhist teachers, group meditation session, food offering to the Buddhas, dedication of merit and a vegetarian meal offered to everyone who comes to the temple. Wat Songdharma Kalyani is also involved in various social work activities.

Situated close to Ratnapaiboon Nunnery, Silacarini Nunnery has three brown-robed nuns called silacarini ("female precept observers"). They observe ten precepts and are in fact samaneri with the exception that they have not received official samaneri ordination. The women received their precepts from the late abbot of Wat Chanasonggram in Bangkok in the 1960s. After his death, the succeeding abbot has refused to continue giving such precepts, which guarantees that the number of silacarini will only decline in the future. These silacarinis lead a quiet and secluded life. They offer religious consultation to the few who seek their help. Their existence is known only to a very limited number of people as they do not involve themselves in outside social work and they seldom appear in public.

Santi Asoke is new Buddhist movement started in the 1960s by Pra Bodhirak. This movement challenges the validity of the existing monks' community and offers a way of life it claims is closer to the teaching of the Buddha and the true spirit of Buddhism. They have a great number of followers, mostly young Buddhists who are dissatisfied with the materialism and consumerism of the existing Sangha.

Within Santi Asoke's ordained community, Pra Bodhirak has also made ordination available to women. However, the highest ranking for women is that of sikhamat, the ten-precept brown-robe nuns. Pra Bodhirak maintains a ratio of four monks to one sikhamat. The number of sikhamats will be limited by the number of monks; at best they can only number one-fourth of the total community. There are approximately twenty sikhamats in this center. They are essentially the same as the original samaneris of the Buddhist tradition. The use of the term "sikhamana" (one who follows the precepts) is purposely avoided, as monks in Thailand are not allowed to give sikhamana ordination.[5]

One branch of Santi Asoke is in Nakhonpathom. Generally, this community follows a very strict routine. The nuns and monks rise before 5 a.m. and are not allowed an afternoon nap. They take only one vegetarian meal a day, and live a lifestyle of extreme simplicity with only the basic necessities. They lead a true communal life, each one having only a small hut with bare requirements. There is a main kitchen where laypeople work together with the monks and nuns. The community attempts to be self-supporting by growing their own vegetables using organic methods. For instance, instead of using chemical insecticides, they cultivate a certain species of flower which acts as a natural insect repellant.

In 1989, Santi Asoke's open support of a particular political party whose success was a threat to incumbent political power led to the movement coming under attack from the traditional Sangha. Bodhirak was charged on the basis that he claimed himself to be enlightened, a claim which, if not true, is considered a defeat for a monk. Bodhirak's lack of Pali knowledge has led to his misinterpretation of certain Buddhist teachings. His propagation of vegetarianism has also come under attack.

Under strong pressure both from the government and the Sangha, Bodhirak was forced to stop wearing the brown robe; he now wears a white robe. All his male followers, arrested along with him, have now changed into loose brown pants with a white robe. The sikhamats have now changed from dark brown robes to gray. The members of Santi Asoke still practice Dharma in a quiet way, and religious activities still go on among the inner group at the center. Among Santi Asoke's sikhamats, many are well-educated, and some speak foreign languages, including French and English. From the standpoint of education, the Santi Asoke nuns are definitely more advanced than many traditional mae jis.

The Sathiendharmasathan Foundation was established by Mae ji Sansanee Sathiensut, age thirty-seven, formerly a successful model and businesswoman who has been a mae ji for over a decade.[6] She does not believe in building temples merely to gain merit, a popular practice. For her, building temples is only a material and physical act. She would rather build good community, and her work, based on this understanding, is designed to train people so that they can follow the rightful path and lead successful, happy lives.

To many, wealth may become an obstacle to Dharma practice. Mae ji Sansanee has used her wealth constructively. She is a nature

constructive use of wealth
in the case of Mae ji Sansanee

lover and her large compound is beautifully arranged with a garden
and lotus pond. The site is used often for training courses, including
a project called Buddhaputra (literally, "sons of the Buddha"), a
three-day training course given twice yearly to high school students.
The training emphasizes giving and sharing as an expression of compassion, the basic teaching of Buddhism. The students are trained to
be able to help those in need, and to learn how to happily give to
others.

The Parents Project is a training project that involves both parents and children. Speakers and trainers are usually monks who try
to impart Buddhist teaching to strengthen family ties and help alle-
viate social problems. The Invalid Children Recovery Project helps
disabled children adapt and cope, and teaches healthy children to
develop compassion and become more concerned for those less fortunate. Another project involves support of the kindergarten school
at Wat Siridhamnimit. In order to help run this school, Mae ji
Sansanee earned a degree in home science. After helping the abbot
set up the school, which includes both a preschool and a kindergarten of over 200 children, she continues to offer regular financial
support.

The Sathiendharmasathan Foundation, primarily financed with
Mae ji Sansanee's personal income, helps generate and fund these
worthy projects. This place is living proof that a wealthy person,
once turned to follow the path of Dharma, can help society im-
mensely. Such opportunity is without gender limitation; men and
women can be equally helpful to the cause of Dharma.

Suankaew Dhamma Center is a branch of Wat Paknam branch,
situated in the Chombung district, Rajburi province. This center
was established when the nunnery at Wat Paknam became over-
crowded. There are approximately twenty mae jis, headed by Mae ji
Wanjai Chookorn, age fifty, one of the many successful disciples of
the famous late abbot of Wat Paknam. Forty acres of land were donated for her project, called "The Mothers' Land." Mae ji Wanjai
Chookorn intends it to be a place for women to live together and
follow the Buddhist path. She herself has been a successful meditation master following the technique of Luang Po Wat Paknam.

Vanasanti Nunnery is situated in Don Yiprom, Petburi province.

Vanasanti Nunnery — self-sufficient + ideal

The unique characteristic of this nunnery is that it is self-support-ing. Vanasanti is headed by Mae ji Thongpien Kaewnaet, age sixty-four.[7] Despite the fact that she has had only four years of primary education, Mae ji Thongpien Kaewnaet has been able to pursue her religious interest. She became a mae ji in her youth and started the nunnery on her own land. A part of the land has been set aside for the main building and residences for thirty mae jis, while the re-mainder is used for agriculture.

Walking around the compound, one cannot help but notice the neat stacks of firewood, and rows of coconut drops drying in the sun to be used later as sugar. All mae jis have their meals together in the large, well-maintained kitchen. The mae jis here practice true com-munal living as intended by the Buddha in the formation of the early communities. Regretfully, this characteristic is not maintained even in some of the major temples.

During the rainy season, mae jis work in the rice field. They keep enough rice for their annual use, while the rest is sold to help main-tain the nunnery. Mae ji Thongpien Kaewnaet, herself from an agri-cultural background, trained her followers to be self-sufficient. After the major rice harvest, the mae jis prepare the soil for beans and other short-term crops. Members of Mae ji Thongpien Kaewnaet's family assist the nunnery by transporting and selling the excess crops in the market.

Women in this small self-supporting nunnery live a quiet commu-nal life and practice Dharma. Their daily routine begins at 5 a.m. with group chanting and meditation, followed by cleaning the com-pound. At 6 a.m., some of the mae jis go out for alms rounds in the nearby villages. Following the traditional pattern, pairs of mae jis are sent in the four directions, a total of eight mae jis. Asked why all thirty mae jis did not go for alms, Mae ji Thongpien Kaewnaet said that the community did not want to become a burden on the villag-ers, so they also cook to feed the rest. All the mae jis share in the responsibility of cooking for the others, and the alms food is shared among the community.

The communal living at this nunnery contrasts with the situation in many other nuns' communities in Thailand. In most, individual mae jis are responsible for their own separate meals, a situation which intensifies the financial differences between them. Vanasanti is successful in introducing communal living because the mae jis work together in the field. The head nun has a developed strong administrative system that binds all the mae jis together as a community. Such a lifestyle is conducive to Dharma practice as it encourages one to let go of individual possessions, and in the long run helps develop an understanding of the Buddhist principle of *anatta* (no-self). This nunnery is a living example of the possibility of a self-supporting Buddhist community for women.

The information on nunneries given here is far from complete. It is only an attempt to provide the reader with a general background. Due to the flexibility in the populations of temples and nunneries, the number of mae jis given is always an approximation; this is true also with the number of monks and novices. During the three-month rainy-season retreat, the number tends to be higher in all temples and nunneries, as it is customary for many laypeople to take temporary ordination for the retreat period.

Larger nunneries are found mainly in central Thailand. Rajburi and Petburi provinces are outstanding for large numbers of mae jis. In the south, there is not a single established nunnery that is worth recording. The low concentration of mae jis in the south is also true for monks, whereas large numbers of monks are found in the northeast, where there are a few well-known meditation masters. The northeast does not boast a large number of mae jis, however, and this difference is still open to further research and study.

Traditionally, temples are meant for monks and novices. When Buddhist women want to lead a religious life at traditional temples, they are usually given a small cell away from the monks' residence, most often in a neglected area of the temple. This situation is generally true for most of the temples where small numbers of mae jis are found. Mae jis receive better quarters only when there are a significant number in residence. It is becoming more popular for mae jis to live in a nunnery completely separated from the temple. There are two major advantages to this: mae jis do not have to attend to cooking and cleaning for the monks, which allows them more time for Dharma study and practice; and they have their own administrative system which is better suited to meet the practical needs of women.

2 advantages of having
nunnery seperate from
temple

[1] Report at the annual meeting on April 7, 1984.

[2] Interview, July 1990.

[3] Including Mae ji Chan of Wat Dhammakaya.

[4] According to this tradition, an abbot or abbess wears a yellow robe, ordinary bhikkhunis wear gray robes, and red robes are worn by high-ranking monks.

[5] See Chapter Five, "Two Bhikkhuni Movements in Thailand," p. 47.

[6] Interviewed on August 27, 1990.

[7] Data collected in 1988.

CHAPTER SEVEN

Prostitutes and Buddhism

As I travel to various international conferences on women and religion, I am often asked questions about prostitution in Thailand. The questions revolve around why there are so many prostitutes in my country, a Buddhist country. Does Buddhism promote prostitution? What does the Sangha say about prostitution? Can a prostitute still be a good Buddhist?

Prostitution has been known in human history from ancient times. It existed in India prior to the Buddha's time. In ancient Greece and Rome, women offered themselves to unknown men at a temple as a form of religious ritual. Money given to them from these encounters was donated directly to the temple, and in this way, it was believed, they gained the favor of the gods. The first house of prostitution was started some 2,600 years ago by Solon, a Greek legalist and social reformer. According to him, the institution of prostitution decreased sexual misbehavior among both men and women. Again, the income from prostitution was given to the temple.[1] Around the fifth century B.C.E., Babylonian women were required to offer their bodies in a temple dedicated to the Goddess Mylitta at least once in their lifetimes as a merit-making ritual.

Although nearly every society condemns prostitution, none has succeeded in completely eradicating it. Apparently, St. Augustine supported prostitution for its functional aspect in making a monogamous society possible. Contemporary sociologists and social theorists differ in their opinions. Some support prostitution as a means of providing men a sexual outlet without much commitment apart from financial gratuity. Others consider prostitution a form of sexual exploitation which denigrates women and treats them solely as a commodity to answer to the sexual needs of men. They see this exploitation in the same nature as exploitation in the labor market. And, they point out that economic and social structures promote prostitution based on the promotion of the idea that women exist for the pleasure of men.

I will begin this discussion by focusing on how prostitution appears in Buddhist texts. Then I will explore the issue of prostitution in contemporary Thai society. Finally, I will examine how Buddhism can help prostitutes.

PROSTITUTES IN EARLY BUDDHIST TEXTS

The term for "prostitute" as found in Buddhist texts is *sobhini*, abbreviated from *nagar sobhini*, meaning a beautiful woman belonging to the city. This title was first given by the king of Vajji, and constituted, in essence, a professional position of state prostitute. To receive this title, a woman, besides being extraordinarily beautiful, had to be learned and well-trained in social arts, such as singing, dancing, conversation, poetry, and the *Kamasutra*, the art of sensual pleasure. Because such a woman was desired by competing kings, princes, and nobles, and could therefore be at the center of conflict that might even escalate into wars, the king bestowed the title of sobhini, meaning that she did not belong to anyone in particular, but could be enjoyed by anyone who could afford the high price of her services. One sobhini was valued at half of the price of the city of Kasi (Varanasi) Apparently, the social status of these women was reasonably high, as they practiced their trade only among upper-caste nobles. Another class of prostitutes served the general public. They were called *ganika*, which simply means a community of women. Ganika were also mentioned in the early Buddhist texts, but the focus was on the sobhini. The early Buddhist texts did not reflect any negative attitude towards prostitutes. The Buddha welcomed these women and gave them the opportunity to walk the path of enlightenment in equality with all people, regardless of gender, caste, or creed.

Ambapali was the sobhini of Vesali. Abandoned as a baby, she was left in the branches of a mango tree—her name means "girl from the mango tree." A gardener found her and brought her to the king of Vesali, and she was raised within the royal compound. A passage in the *Khuddhaka Nikaya* describes her beauty: "She has jet black and shiny hair, her eyebrows are as beautiful as drawn by the hand of a great artist. Her two legs are those of ivory, her feet as soft as cotton." The *Mahavagga* goes on to state that the rate for her services

68

was as high as fifty *kahapanas* for a night, and that she was well versed in the "sixty-four arts" of seducing and pleasing men of noble families.

Various princes and kings of Vesali wanted to own her, and when they could not settle their disputes over her, they gave her the title of sobhini. Ambapali was to serve them at a set rate. Later, King Bimbisara of Rajagaha took her as his consort, and a son was born to them. Their son, Vimala Kondañña, later joined the Sangha and became enlightened.

The *Ambapali Theriyapadana* narrates the story of Ambapali's previous births. Once she was born into the *ksatriya* (warrior) caste, as the younger sister of the Venerable Pussamuni. She practiced well in Dharma and merit making, and her wish to be born beautiful in her next life came true when she was born in a Brahman family. However, proud of her own beauty, she cursed and insulted a bhikkhuni. This action sent her through many suffering lives, and she was born many times as a prostitute. At the time of the previous Buddha Kassapa, she was ordained and became a bhikkhuni. After that she was born and resided in Tritimsa heaven. Then, in the time of the Gotama Buddha, she was born in her last birth as a prostitute.

In the *Maha Parinibbana Sutta*, we are told of the time that the Buddha stopped and rested in a mango grove belonging to Ambapali. She paid him respect and invited him and his followers for lunch the next day. A group of Licchavi nobles, who also wanted to offer lunch to the Buddha on the same day, offered her 100,000 kahapanas if she would withdraw her invitation. When Ambapali refused, the nobles approached the Buddha directly, but he informed them that he had already accepted Ambapali's invitation. When the Buddha went for lunch at her place the next day, she offered her mango grove to the Buddha and the Sangha. Later she gave up her belongings, renounced her former life, and became a bhikkhuni. She practiced Dharma diligently, became enlightened, and was a skilled Dharma propagator for many years.

Salavati was another famous sobhini of Vesali.[2] She was beautiful and learned, well-versed in the arts of singing, dancing, and entertaining men. To spend a night with her cost a minimum of 100 kahapanas. Her first child, Jivaka, was raised by Prince Abhyaraja, son of King Bimbisara of Rajagaha. Later he left the palace, went to Taxila to study medicine, and became the physician of the Buddha and the Sangha.

Salavati's second child, Sirima, was very beautiful and capable, and she became a sobhini after her mother. She was a devout Buddhist who made daily offerings to a group of eight monks. One young monk, hearing about her beauty, desired to see her. He went to receive dana at her house. On that particular day she was ill, and appeared unadorned to make her routine offerings to the monks. Thinking that even unadorned she was beautiful, and how much more beautiful would she be with fine adornments, this young monk became obsessed with Sirima and was filled with desire for her.

Soon after this incident, Sirima passed away and the Buddha requested to keep her body for four days. On the fourth day he went to the funeral pyre with a retinue of monks including the young monk who had been infatuated with her. The Buddha made an offering of her body, starting with a price of 1,000 kahapanas, and lowering the price down to one, yet no one wanted her body. The Buddha then went on to explain the impermanence of the body. Deeply affected by the Buddha's teaching, the young monk soon entered the path of non-returner.[3]

How did the texts explain the cause of prostitution? We have already seen how the *Ambapali Theriyapadana* related the previous births of Ambapali. Here is a story of Addhakasi, who became a sobhini due to her previous karma. In the time of the Buddha Kassapa, she was a bhikkhuni. In anger, she cursed her bhikkhuni friend, calling her a prostitute. Because of this she suffered through many lives. In her last birth, she was born into a wealthy family, but because of her beauty she was given the title of sobhini. Addhakasi had heard the teaching of the Buddha and later joined the Sangha. To be ordained, she had to travel from Kasi to Savatthi, but some thieves on the highway were planning to abduct her. Knowing this, the Buddha, for the first time, allowed ordination through a messenger. Addhakasi soon became enlightened and helped propagate the teaching of the Buddha from her own experience.

In the *Therigatha* or *Psalms of the Buddhist Sisters*, there is a record of Vimalapurana Ganika, a beautiful sobhini who later joined the

Sangha and became enlightened. Her verse on understanding the true nature of attachment is preserved in the *Therigatha*.

Before turning to look at the problems of prostitution in the contemporary world, it might be worthwhile to examine the Buddhist attitude towards prostitution. On a primary level, Buddhism does not deny prostitutes equal opportunity for enlightenment. Some of the leading prostitutes progressed rapidly on the path because of the fact that they were prostitutes, having experienced the extremes of sensual indulgence and realized the meaninglessness of it.

But the prostitution of the Buddha's time was entirely different from the prostitution prevalent in modern society. Prostitution, then, was a profession of upper-caste society. Prostitutes circulated among nobles, and had a relatively high social standing. However, the very existence of prostitution, then and now, owes much to male greed and lust. When they could not agree among themselves about sexual ownership of a particular woman, they made her public property; she did not really belong to anyone, yet she belonged to all. As we have seen in Indian culture, women are treated as mere objects to be possessed by male owners. A woman's fate was determined by men's power in politics, society, religion, and economics. Women today still face this predicament.

Buddhism does not deny the spiritual potential that prostitutes share with all of humanity. But Buddhism does not promote or encourage prostitution. Instead, it suggests that it is a type of existence characterized by suffering. As we have seen, Buddhist texts say that being born a prostitute is the result of karma.

There were cases of prostitutes who, after accepting Buddhism, followed a life of purity and gave up prostitution. Although Buddhism is open to prostitutes, it does not support prostitution. To the contrary, it helps to strengthen women so that they can give up prostitution and lead better lives.

PROSTITUTES IN THAILAND

In Thailand, prostitution was mentioned during King Rama I's reign.[4] There was taxation of prostitutes and brothels called "tax for the road." When Rama V abolished slavery, some female slaves were turned over to men who started brothels. Prostitution was legalized in 1934 by Rama V. He expressed his concern about prostitutes who worked in gangs with men as their supervisors. The situation was prone to violence, and the threat of spreading venereal disease was great. Because of these dangers, Rama V allowed prostitutes to be registered so that they could receive regular medical care.[5]

At first, the rule applied only to prostitutes in Bangkok, but when it was found that prostitution was also prevalent in the rural provinces, the act was extended to the entire country. Rama V's act dealt directly with prostitution and the prevention of venereal disease, and attempted to protect women from being forced into prostitution. But there was no attempt to help prostitutes free themselves from the trade, nor any attempt to elevate the lives of prostitutes.

Thailand remained under this act until 1960, when the United Nations declared the abolition of prostitution. The Thai government answered the UN policy by introducing "The Act to Deter Prostitution," replacing the 1934 law. According to this new act, no one is permitted to perform in the sex trade, either heterosexual or homosexual. A person who has transgressed the law will be fined a maximum of 2,000 *baht* (about $80 U.S.) or sentenced to imprisonment for up to two months.

Through this act, prostitution became illegal, which is to say, from the legal point of view, there are no prostitutes. Chalermpol Satthaporn, who has done research on prostitution in Thailand, found that after legal prohibition the number of prostitutes increased noticeably.[6] Before the Act, 15% of prostitutes were between the ages of fifteen and nineteen, but after the declaration of the Act, the percentage increased to 25%. Also more women from rural areas became prostitutes. In provinces where there were military bases, the number of prostitutes also noticeably increased. Satthaporn also found that after the Act to Deter Prostitution, the number of people who were sentenced to imprisonment on charges of sexual harassment increased rapidly.[7]

Thailand's prostitution industry escalated dramatically during the 1960s when the United States established military bases here during the Vietnam War. Even after the bases were dismantled, prostitution continued to spread in various guises—bar-girls, singers, partners, and other "cover" occupations. Thailand has sacrificed its women along with social and cultural values for a short-lived economic boom.

Statistics on the number of prostitutes has always been controversial between government organizations, on the one hand, and non-government organizations, on the other. Because prostitution is illegal, there is no official record of prostitutes. Morris G. Fox, a United Nations consultant on social welfare who did a study on prostitution in 1957, reported 20,000 prostitutes, half in Bangkok.[8] Dr. Pasuk Pongpaichit, an economics professor at Chulalongkorn University, says that the current number of prostitutes is between 700,000 to one million.[9] This figure is generally accepted by many organizations dealing with the problem of prostitution. This includes approximately 200,000 Thai prostitutes working abroad. Pasuk gives a regional breakdown: 43% from the north, 26% from the northeast, 20% from central Thailand, and 4% from the south.

The prostitution industry is spread throughout various "professions." Arathai Dilok-Udomchai reported that 41% of the prostitutes worked in restaurants, 20% in brothels, 13% in hotels, 11% in rented houses, 3.8% in barbershops, 2.5% in bars and 1.3% in massage parlors.[10]

The majority of prostitutes have only four years of primary education, only a quarter had reached grade seven, and the remaining women have had no formal education at all.[11]

Both Sunee Malligmalaya and Dilok-Udomchai reported that the majority of women became prostitutes at age sixteen. Malligmalaya found the age range between sixteen and nineteen is a high percentage in both voluntary (44%) and involuntary (64%) prostitutes, and pointed out the correlation between younger age range and greater number of prostitutes.[12] Wongchai's informants were mainly women who had experience working in foreign countries, and therefore reported a slightly older age range: twenty-seven to twenty-nine, (24%); thirty to thirty-two, (26%).[13]

The majority of prostitutes come from agricultural families who have no financial guarantee of their annual product. The majority of these families work on borrowed land.[14] Dilok-Udomchai found that 50% of her study cases were from agricultural backgrounds, 22.54% were from labor, and 15.45% were from families owning small businesses. Malligmalaya found that 60% of voluntary and

80% of involuntary prostitutes came from agricultural backgrounds. Wongchai also reported that the highest percentage of her informants came from agricultural backgrounds (56%). This finding reflects the need for the government to pay serious attention to the standard of living of farmers, who comprise the majority of the Thai population. Prostitution may be seen partly as the result of Thailand's unsuccessful agricultural system.

Another finding which is important to consider is that prostitutes usually come from large families, with an average of six to eight children. Often prostitutes are the eldest children in the families. Wongchai reported that 53% of her informants have between six to ten siblings, a finding corroborated by Dilok-Udomchai's study. Malligmalaya found that prostitutes usually came from families of six to seven children.[15] This probably reflects the inability of the parents to support such a large family. The young women who became prostitutes, as the eldest children, were made to bear a heavy financial burden to see their families through.

HEALTH

Prostitutes also face physical and mental difficulties. Wongchai's report gives the following statistics for common health problems encountered by the women in her study: 58% had venereal disease; 75% were addicted to cigarettes; 32% used sexual stimulants; 49% often had headaches; 41% had trouble sleeping. A more recent and frightening health problem was studied by Meechai Veeravaidhya, who quoted the following statistics of AIDS among prostitutes in Chiengrai (which has a high concentration of prostitutes). In 1987 there were no reported cases; in 1988, 0.98% of the prostitutes were diagnosed; in 1989, 36%; by August of 1990, 56% of the total population of prostitutes were diagnosed as HIV positive.[16]

Fabrizio Ossella, deputy regional representative of the UN Development Program warned that Thailand is "...on the verge of a great tragedy." A report from the Division of Epidemiology said that 100,000 Thais might already be infected with Human Immuno-deficiency Virus (HIV), the harbinger of AIDS. Ossello urged: "The Thai Government must mobilize many more resources...immediate action must be taken by all, I repeat, all ministries. The strength of the HIV infection cannot be held in check by the Ministry of Public Health by itself."[17]

Considering the rapid spread of AIDS among the prostitutes of Chiengrai, and the high total number of prostitutes in Thailand (700,000 to one million), one realizes that we are not talking of a threat to prostitutes only, but to the whole nation. This situation is so critical that Meechai warned, "we are not talking about [a] health problem [only]...we are now dealing with the death of the nation." ✕

INCOME

The income that prostitutes earn for their services varies according to preferences for age and physical beauty. Malligmalaya reported that the highest rate is 6,000 baht (about $240) for the service of first-time prostitutes. Generally, 51% of the prostitutes receive less than 500 baht ($20) and 36% receive less than 100 baht ($4). In general, the prostitutes themselves actually receive less than one-third of what the customers pay.

Prostitution is carried out under various guises, occurring among bar-girls, night club singers, girls working in barbershops, waitresses working in restaurants, and even university and college students. Wongchai has classified different types of prostitutes. As prostitution is illegal, publicly known prostitutes must go in hiding to avoid arrest during police raids. "Half-known" prostitutes are those who themselves view their trade as prostitution, such as "call-girls," but are not generally publicly known as such. A third category is women who work as prostitutes under "cover" jobs, such as bar-girls, "partners," women working in massage parlors, etc. Touring prostitutes are another class of prostitute. They travel to large cities, tourist resorts, and the like, meet their clients in big hotels, and then move on to other cities. This makes them difficult to locate and record, as they tend to change their trade names as they move from town to town. Another category is legally married prostitutes whose husbands often work as pimps providing protection and cover, and live on their wives' income. Temporary prostitutes turn to prostitution due to an immediate financial crisis or lack of economic support. They give up the profession as soon as they are financially stable. [18]

Wongchai did a study on women working as prostitutes in foreign

high #s of prostitutes from Thailand due not solely to poverty levels

countries. Due to legal restrictions, these women found themselves working as prostitutes under cover jobs: "go-go" dancers, sex show performers, bar-hostesses, night club workers, actresses in porno-graphic films, and others.[19] Japan is considered the best place for the sex-trade, offering the highest income for people in this business.[20] The majority of prostitutes working abroad are from northern Thailand, ranging from sixteen to twenty-five years of age. Their average income is between $800-$1,200 a month, from which $200-$240 will be deducted. They work abroad for periods of six to nine months. Each year about five hundred women are deported back to Thailand for illegal entry into foreign countries.

West Germany has an annual entry of 2,000 Thai prostitutes, and Hong Kong has the same number. Thai prostitutes started to work in Brunei four to five years ago, working from one to two weeks each trip, and averaging about $200 a day. Each trip they earn from $2,800 up to a maximum of $6,000, depending on special services or popularity. Prior to the Gulf War, Iraq was also a lucrative destination in the Middle East. Thai prostitutes there earned from $800 to $1,200 monthly.

It is commonly believed that poverty is the sole cause of prostitution in Thailand. However, statistical evidence does not necessarily bear this out. For instance, the northeast is the poorest region of the country. If poverty is the sole cause of prostitution, the number of prostitutes from the northeast should be the highest. However, this is not so: all studies found that many more women from the north became prostitutes than women of other regions. Careful study reveals more complex causes forcing women into prostitution.

However, economic factors are a major cause of prostitution. The majority of prostitutes come from agricultural backgrounds, from families without economic stability. In some years, their families' agricultural yield is enough only to meet basic survival needs. Other families work on rented land and have to return half the yield to the landowners. What remains is not sufficient to meet expenses, such as for pesticides and farm equipment, some of which is acquired on loan. Some farming families soon find themselves in substantial debt, far beyond their ability to repay.

Linked with economic instability and poverty is lack of education.

The majority of prostitutes have had only four years of compulsory education. Farmers who have to struggle to survive economically will not be able to provide higher education for their children. Many farmers, being poor and uneducated themselves, do not have proper knowledge of family planning, and as a result have large families which create an added economic burden so serious that it falls also to the eldest daughters in the families to help out. This explains the high percentage of prostitutes who have many siblings, and are themselves the eldest daughters. Economic factors cause further problems: the break-up of the families; husbands deserting wives and children; and great numbers of rural poor who come to seek jobs in Bangkok, often with little success, as most of them are unskilled.

Government policy in economic development promotes only material and industrial growth. It pays little attention to the social and cultural values of the country. The promotion of tourism, for example, is little more than the promotion of prostitution. The Government quotes successful economic growth from the rapid increase of the National Income Per Capita, in which the high income from prostitution is included. Thai prostitutes working abroad send home as much as 1.2 million dollars each year.

Social factors interrelated with economics are also responsible for prostitution. We have seen how economic factors affect the educational standard of rural farmers and their children, and the connection between poverty, lack of education, and prostitution. Malligmalaya found the highest percentage of prostitution occurs in the age range between ten and nineteen years old. She pointed out that girls at this age should still be in school, but due to lack of financial support they have to leave school and enter the labor market without skills, with an average of only four years of formal education.[21] With no other significant option for financial stability, these young girls are forced into prostitution.

Young women, tired of living in rural poverty with no future, find themselves ready and willing to take a chance at a new life promised by agents, who tactfully approach the girls' parents. Many of these young women have already been exposed to the dream of living in luxury as fed to them through television and other mass media. They want beautiful things and an easy lifestyle. Prostitution seems to them to be the only means available to actualize their dreams. Among teenagers especially, it is very popular to follow the lead of one's peer group and friends. Dilok-Udomchai found that 37% of the prostitutes joined the sex trade because they went along with the pattern set by their friends.

Negative social values that denigrate women also contribute to the problem of prostitution in Thailand. Another aspect is the great emphasis Thai society places on virginity, which is to be preserved for one's husband. This overemphasized value has backfired. Among rape cases, for example, young girls think that once they have lost their virginity, they have no value, and so they believe their only option is to become a prostitute.

Other girls become prostitutes out of a sense of duty or obligation to their parents, to share the family's economic burden. When the family is in great debt resulting from failure in agricultural production, or even simply from the father's gambling losses, the eldest daughters are asked to "sacrifice" for their parents and their younger siblings. There are cases where fathers sold and re-sold their daughters into prostitution to buy extra cows for farming. This is done in the belief that children must show "gratitude" to their parents.

It is interesting to note the resemblance in the reasoning of both prostitutes and mae jis for their life choices. Due to "gratitude" or obligation, some women become prostitutes to repay their parents materially, while others choose to become mae jis to repay their parents spiritually, offering them the merit of their religious activities.

Many Thai proverbs reflect the values that relegate women to the status of a commmodity or an object of male desire. A woman is compared to a flower, for example, while a man is described as an insect. In the north there is a saying that encourages women to pay attention to their outer appearance more than to what they eat, as no one can see what is inside their stomachs. These images result in women overemphasizing their physical beauty as their primary worth. Many Thai women spend their spare time and money beautifying themselves in order to maintain this projected image, even at the expense of their own mental and spiritual development. We have even seen cases of girls who became prostitutes simply because they wanted to own beautiful clothes.

♂ Thai values regarding sexuality, ♀...
feed prostitution
→ harks back to Brahmanical values

Prostitutes and Buddhism

The great majority of men in Thailand still cling to the sexist, Brahmanical social values that came to Thailand in the Ayudhya period. A "true man" must be good at fighting and at winning women. Even today, many Thai men still buy charms and amulets to help them gain sexual access to women. Then, after "winning" a woman, they often move along to seek another sexual challenge. There is a saying that warns women against men who work with the railway company, the ferry company, as local dancers and stage performers, and as policemen. This is because these men tend to be on the move all the time, and have gained a notorious reputation for leaving behind their marital responsibilities as well.

It is common practice for Thai men to visit brothels to prove their virility. Men who do not do so are considered strange and suffer the possibility of becoming social outcasts. Many men say that they cannot break the habit of going to prostitutes because they are so readily available and are a cheap source of entertainment. Too many Thai women also accept prostitution as a commonplace practice, and some who do not wish to have a sexual relationship with their husbands have even encouraged them to see prostitutes. Now, with the spread of AIDS, child prostitution is further promoted in the belief that young girls are free from the dangerous disease.

SOLUTIONS

In this chapter, we have seen how prostitution, from its early form as a religious ritual developed and degenerated into an international "flesh trade" that destroys the value of women as human beings. To discuss solutions to what has become a great human disease seems almost impossible, but the following are some proposals for addressing Thailand's prostitution problem.

The Thai government must have a clear and systematic policy regarding prostitutes. They must collect and maintain up-to-date data and develop greater sensitivity in dealing with the problem. Legal structures need to be strengthened so that women are protected from exploitation by providing opportunities in education, health care, and security.

National development must be planned with a long-range view, to develop the nation in every sphere of life, not just economically and materially. The well-being of Thailand's population depends on a strong society with moral and ethical standards that elevate rather than denigrate people. Overemphasis on economic and material development at the expense of mental and spiritual development push women, whose options are already limited in society, towards prostitution as the only way to actualize their material desires.

Religious organizations and authorities must begin to show concern for the existing problems faced by women. Negative social values against women and values promoting prostitution must be critically examined and corrected by religious authorities. Silence from religious authorities can be taken as indirect responsibility for prostitution. All means to elevate the status of women must be promoted, including opening up the religious sphere to more participation by women. Individually, members of the Sangha and religious institutions can act as strong moral exemplars to Thai society. Buddhist temples can also provide temporary shelter for destitute women, the same way that the temples have traditionally served this function for Thai men.

On March 8, 1989, various women's groups, including the Friends of Women, the Women's Foundation, Women Writers and Reporters, Empower, the Association for the Promotion of Women's Status, the Women's Development Institute, the Y.W.C.A., and the Independent Women's Group, made a joint statement in an open letter to the Thai government, attacking its policy of using prostitution to boost tourism and the economy as reflecting a lack of any real understanding of human dignity and women's self-esteem.[22] The open letter also called for the following acts:

> 1. The abolition of the Prostitution Control Bill, which treats prostitutes as criminals and prescribes "less stringent punishment for procurers and brothel operators than the Criminal Law: [an] incongruency [that] leads to a selective use of the law by law enforcers."

> 2. The establishment of a committee which is empowered to inspect sex-related enterprises.

> 3. The abolition of procedures that empower the police to keep records on prostitutes. Such a practice treats women as

criminals and the record should be transferred to the Labor Department instead.

4. A strictly enforced law that permits no girls under 18 to work in sex-related businesses.

5. Punishment for customers and operators of sex businesses in cases where girls are found to be under 18.

6. Non-formal occupational training for rural young people to prevent them from entering the sex trade and to provide skills to former prostitutes who wish to seek alternative work.

7. A public campaign to warn rural villagers that in the future they stand to be heavily punished for selling their children.

8. The establishment of a committee to study prostitution-related problems and their solutions from economic and social points of view, and to consider the legal aspects of these problems.

BUDDHISM AND PROSTITUTION

The teachings of Buddhism can be effective tools in coping with the problem of prostitution. Buddhist history and tradition have set an example for us. Many well-known prostitutes during the time of the Buddha benefited from the teaching, and their understanding of Buddhism led them to give up prostitution. Some joined the Sangha as bhikkhunis and excelled in spiritual development. Some became enlightened and a strong force for the propagation of Buddhism.

As a Buddhist, one takes refuge in the Buddha, the Dharma, and the Sangha. Does the Triple Gem (*Triratna*) offer refuge to prostitutes? The Buddha set examples in his own life with the positive attitude he held towards prostitutes. The Buddha came in direct contact with prostitutes many times. He and his community benefited directly by accepting dana from them on numerous occasions.

The Buddha felt a responsibility to help all sentient beings to spiritual salvation. Prostitutes were treated like any other suffering, sentient being when they came to the Buddha for refuge. Even though the historical Buddha is gone, Buddhist teaching encourages us to help ourselves through following the examples he set for us.

The teachings of the Buddha are directly relevant to prostitutes. They can be of great help, not only in freeing women from prostitution but also in nurturing them on the spiritual path.

The Buddha accepted his aunt, Mahapajapati Gotami, to join the Sangha in the conviction that all human beings are equally capable of spiritual achievement. This was the first time in the history of world religion that a male religious leader made such a clear, unmitigated recognition of female spiritual potential. Buddhist women must understand the importance of this recognition and use it well. Spiritual equality means that the path to enlightenment is open to all, *without exception*.

The first Noble Truth taught by the Buddha was *dukkha*, that life is suffering. Whatever one's social role or position, one experiences this suffering. Only when one realizes this and begins to seek a way out, does the teaching of Buddhism become meaningful. If a prostitute begins to understand her own suffering, she can seek to improve her lot by following the path shown by the Buddha.

Nirvana, the highest spiritual goal of Buddhists, is available to all. The purity or impurity of the body cannot prevent one from realizing this highest truth. Prostitutes, despite the fact that they are condemned by society, can use their life experience to great advantage on the spiritual path. There were cases of prostitutes in the Buddha's time who made a complete turn towards religious lives because they had experienced extremes of indulgence and degradation, and realized the utter meaninglessness of it.

The teachings of the three characteristics of conditioned existence (*Trilaksana*)—*dukkha* (suffering), *anicca* (impermanence), and *anatta* (no-self)—are especially valuable. Everything in this phenomenal world is marked by these three characteristics. The nature of impermanence is especially relevant for prostitutes, whose livelihood depends on physical beauty and youth, which are fleeting. The teaching of Buddhism may help them understand that placing great value on physical and sensual experiences that are impermanent only leads to greater suffering.

But Buddhist teaching may not always be perfectly reflected in the Buddhist institution, the Sangha. There are prevalent attitudes that continue to lead Thai society to see prostitutes, and women in general, in a negative light. "Sangha" traditionally means the community of monks and nuns. A group of four or more monks and nuns is considered Sangha. In the West, the term often includes the lay Buddhist community. In the Theravada tradition, however, use of the term "Sangha" is reserved for ordained people. As there are no officially recognized nuns in Thailand, Sangha in Thailand means only the community of monks.

We need to have a clear understanding of the nature of the Thai Sangha. The requirements for a man to join the Sangha are minimal. Virtually any man off the street can become a monk, provided he is not completely blind, severely deformed, or obviously insane. There is no requirement for an educational standard—the majority of Thai monks have only four years of compulsory education (the same as most mae jis). Unlike the Christian tradition, Buddhist men become monks first, and then study Buddhism. A great many monks do not continue a formal Buddhist education. Many monks are simply uneducated farmers in yellow robes.

These facts do not have much social impact in themselves. But the actual situation in Thailand is that Thai society holds the Sangha in extremely high regard, seeing them as representing directly the Buddha. Whatever monks do, good or bad, laypeople prefer not to interfere, being afraid to lose merit and create negative personal karma by speaking ill of monks. A local saying, "Bad is up to the nuns, and good is up to the monks," expresses clearly Thai laypeople's belief that whatever the Sangha does is entirely up to them (and that its female members can be expected to be the source of "badness"). This is a very harmful attitude and is far removed from the spirit of early Buddhism, where the Sangha and the laity were mutually supportive. The Sangha was expected to provide spiritual guidance, and to uphold Buddhist values in their behavior, while it was the role of the laity to provide material support in exchange. The lay community was also in a position to check the moral standard of the Sangha, as evidenced in early Buddhist texts.

Within the context of the Thai Sangha, we should not be surprised to find cases of monks who emphasize the inferiority of women and the evil karma of prostitutes. They can then suggest that women and prostitutes should make more merit to guarantee better

THAI WOMEN IN BUDDHISM

future lives by offering dana to the temple. As a result, some temples in the north are richly adorned from the income of prostitutes.

The Sangha may still be meaningful to village life in rural Thailand, but in large urban areas like Bangkok, the tie between the Sangha and the lay community is very fragile. The Sangha, for the most part, fulfills only public ceremonial or ritualistic needs. For too long there has been no intellectual dialogue between the Sangha and the lay community at any meaningful level. There is a great need for the Sangha to revitalize the structure of Buddhist education in order to strengthen, at very least, its own monks, so that they can provide effective spiritual guidance for the great numbers of people living in cities.

While the number of prostitutes has dramatically increased in the past two or three decades, the number of monks and novices has remained the same, around 300,000. The Sangha maintains a very reserved attitude toward social issues in general, including the issue of prostitution. This social denial is partly due to the understanding, or misunderstanding, that the Sangha should not interfere in the "worldly concerns" of laypeople. With such an attitude, it is indeed difficult to expect any meaningful or constructive involvement from the Sangha.

Some Buddhists are known to make a distinction and take refuge only in the Ariya Sangha, that is, the community of enlightened monks. So when we take refuge in the Sangha, we laypeople must be aware of its nature and shortcomings. We must be careful not to accept and follow blindly the advice of often uneducated monks.

Bhikkhunis in the West have been doing wonderful work for society. For rape victims and women who have had abortions, bhikkhunis can perform religious rituals that help to reestablish them mentally and spiritually. This has a great psychological effect on women who have experienced trauma and suffering. Ven. Sangye Khadro, an American nun ordained in the Tibetan tradition, has suggested purification practices involving four steps, by adopting four mental attitudes: regret, refuge, resolution, and counter-measure. By generating these four states of mind sincerely with compassion, women can help to heal the pain and guilt experienced after an abortion.[23] But true healing or purification comes with learning to be more open and loving towards all beings, acknowledging their right to live and be happy. Buddhist teaching and practice can also be similarly applied to prostitutes, to help them change their lives for the better.

To cope with prostitution, there is a great need for the reintroduction of the Bhikkhuni Sangha. Nuns would be better able to advise and offer spiritual guidance to other women. Buddhist temples have traditionally served another "hidden" function as "half-way houses" for destitute people. But because there are only monks in Thailand, this social service is limited to men. Sulak Sivaraksa, a well-known Thai Buddhist social critic, has said that the lack of the Bhikkhuni Sangha in Thailand is partly responsible for the high growth of prostitution. Raising women in temples will lessen the number of women in brothels; providing religious space for women will help lessen social ills.[24]

As we have seen in our discussion, various social and political issues are interdependently linked in the problem of prostitution. I am convinced that Buddhism can be of great help to prostitutes, provided the Thai Buddhist Sangha and government officials are willing to undergo a fundamental shift towards a clear understanding of the problem. There is a great need for willingness on the part of all people concerned to recognize the nature of these problems so that they can plan for effective solution.

There exists a great need for the Thai Buddhist Sangha to come out of its protective shell and become more involved directly in helping women, and indirectly by deepening its own understanding of Buddhism. If the fear of women becoming equal to men is at the base of the Sangha's unwillingness to change its ways, it should know that according to the teachings of the Buddha, women are already equal to men in spiritual potential, spiritual development, and accomplishment. Social problems are so pressing and urgent that there is no time to waste. For effective social change in Thailand, everyone, regardless of gender, class, or ethnicity, must learn to cooperate. We all must realize and actualize our unlimited human potential, in order for our children to live in a world better than the one we can now offer them.

1 Quoted by Panna Ruck-urai, "Social Welfare for Some Categories of Women in Thailand" (Unpublished paper, Chulalongkorn University, Bangkok, 1959), p. 132.

2 Max Muller, ed., and H. Oldenburg, trans., *Mahavagga, Vinaya Pitaka*, Vol. XIII, *Sacred Books of the East* (Delhi: Motilal Banarsidass, 1965).

3 *Khuddaka Nikaya, Tripitaka for the People*. Edited by Sujeeb Buññanbarp. (Bangkok: Terd Toon Tham Group, 1979).

4 *Kot Mai Tra Sam Duang* (Bangkok: Gurusabha Press, 1962), part 1.

5 "Prevention of Venereal Disease Act B.E. 2477," *Pramuan Kot Mai Prajamsok* (1934), p. 345.

6 Chalermpol Satthaporn, "Problems of Prostitutes in Thailand" (Unpublished M.A. thesis, Faculty of Political Science, Thammasat University, Bangkok), 1965, p. 94.

7 *Ibid.*, p. 31.

8 Quoted in *Ibid.*, p. 12.

9 Quoted by Yupa Wongchai in "Economic and Social Factors Affecting Thai Women's Determination in Practicing Prostitution Abroad" (Unpublished, funded by the Committee of National Research,1988).

10 Arathai Dilok-Udomchai, "Expectation on Social Context Effecting Self Adjustment: Case Study on Women at Kred Trakarn Welfare Home, July 1986-March 1987" (Unpublished M.A. thesis, Faculty of Social Welfare, Thammasat University, Bangkok, 1987), p. 120.

11 Dilok-Udomchai, *Op. Cit.*, p. 64, and Wongchai, *Op. Cit.*, p. 40.

12 Sunee Malligmalaya, et al., "Legal and Other Measures to Cope with Problems of Prostitution in Thailand" (National Research Institute, 1982).

13 Wongchai, *Op. Cit.*, p. 40.

14 Malligmalaya, *Op. Cit.*,p. 59.

15 *Ibid.*, p. 52.

16 Quoted at a seminar on "The Role of Government and Non-Government Organizations in Preventing and Correcting Sexual Business Service," held September 18-19, 1990 at the Santi-Maitri Building, Government House, Bangkok.

17 Ossella Fabrizio in *The Nation*, Bangkok, September 27, 1990.

18 Wongchai, *Op. Cit.*, p. 11.

19 *Ibid.*, p. 29.

20 *Ibid.*, p. 17.

21 Malligmalaya, *Op. Cit.*, p. 180.

22 Sanitsuda Ekachai, "Bouquets and Brickbat[s] for Policy on Women," in the *Bangkok Post*, March 8, 1989.

23 Ven. Sangye Khadro, "Buddhist Views on Abortion," in *NIBWA* no. 17, October-December 1988.

24 At Thammasat University, 1988.

CHAPTER EIGHT

Buddhist Nuns in Other Countries

In this chapter, the reader is provided with a global context in order to compare the situation of Thai women with that of Buddhist
women in other countries.[1]

SRI LANKA

Sri Lanka has a unique place in the history of Buddhist nuns. It was
the first country outside of India in which the Bhikkhuni Sangha
was established. In the third century B.C.E., King Asoka's son, Prince
Mahinda Thera, traveled to Sri Lanka with a retinue of Buddhist
monks to teach Buddhism there. While he was there, the Sri Lankan
king's sister-in-law Anula requested ordination from Mahinda
Thera. He explained to her the rule that both Sanghas had to be
present at the ordination of bhikkhunis. Mahinda suggested that
King Devananpiyatissa send an envoy to India requesting King
Asoka to send his daughter, the learned nun Sanghamitta Theri.

Subsequently, King Asoka sent Sanghamitta Theri, accompanied
by a group of learned bhikkhuni theris. The group was well received
by the royal family of Sri Lanka, and ordination was given not only
to Queen Anula, but also to five hundred female attendants. The
King had a separate nunnery built, called Bhikkhunupasaya. This
marked the establishment of the bhikkhuni lineage in Sri Lanka
which prospered alongside the Bhikkhu Sangha. Throughout their
history in Sri Lanka, both Sanghas received regular royal support.
The bhikkhunis were active in their Dharma study, and there is evidence that they were also involved in social welfare activities, such
as running a hospital.[2]

In 433 C.E., a group of Chinese women requested help from the
Sri Lankan Sangha in establishing a Bhikkhuni Sangha. A group of
Sri Lankan bhikkhunis, led by Bhikkhuni Devasara, went to China
and gave ordination to three hundred Chinese women in Nanking,
establishing a lineage that is still in existence today.[3]

In Sri Lanka, however, the Bhikkhuni Sangha survived for only a thousand years after its establishment, after which it disappeared together with the Bhikkhu Sangha, when the Chola dynasty of South India invaded and overthrew the Sri Lankan kingdom. The Sri Lankan Sangha suffered great losses during this violent encroachment from the Hindu Cholas, and many temples were destroyed. When the country was restored, there was only one Buddhist novice left on the whole island. The Sri Lankans invited bhikkhus from Thailand to reestablish the monks' order, but as there were no bhikkhunis in Thailand, the nuns' order was never reestablished in Sri Lanka.

In 1880, Catherine de Alwis, a European Anglican woman from Sri Lanka, became a Buddhist and later was ordained in Burma as Sister Sudharma. She returned to Sri Lanka in 1905, and established an *aramaya* (hermitage) which also housed orphaned or abandoned children, and aged or destitute women. At first, only women over age forty were allowed ordination, but after 1920 younger women were also accepted.

Such nuns are called *dasa silamata* ("ten-precept mother") or *sil maniyo*. They shave their heads and wear yellow robes, but without the patch-work characteristic of monks' robes. Although they observe ten precepts they are, like Thailand's mae jis, not samaneris but technically laypeople, a very ambiguous position.

Today there are at least 2,500 silamatas throughout the island. The actual number may be higher, but some refuse to register with the government for fear they will be punished in some way. They are generally very poor and live in small aramayas, sometimes only one or two silamatas in a group. In 1984, Sister Ayya Khema, a German woman who became a silamata after taking the precepts from a Buddhist thera in Sri Lanka, started an International Buddhist Women's Center on Parappuduwa Island. Ayya Khema was influential among upper-class Sri Lankan women and was well supported by them, but political unrest has curtailed her activities on the island. Ayya Khema went to Los Angeles and received bhikkhuni ordination in 1988 along with five other silamatas from Sri Lanka.

This might have been the beginning of reestablishing the Sri Lankan Bhikkhuni Sangha. However, the general attitude of the Sri

Lankan people in regard to the the bhikkhuni issue has been as negative and unsupportive as in Thailand. Despite the fact that Sri Lankan bhikkhunis once gave ordination to Chinese women, Sri Lankan bhikkhus still object to the idea of receiving the lineage back from the Chinese Bhikkhuni Sangha, which they consider to be Mahayana.

The Sri Lankan government shows much more concern towards the situation of silamatas than the Thai government has shown towards mae jis. They have attempted to set up a system of registering silamatas and issuing identity cards. The Minister of Cultural Affairs has sent representatives to China to obtain information regarding the Chinese lineage, and a representative was sent to participate in and observe the first conference of Buddhist nuns in India in 1987. Recently, there has also been an attempt to provide education for silamatas, and in the long run, one can expect a slow improvement of their situation. Society will take heed when silamatas are able to prove themselves worthwhile and beneficial to society.

BURMA

Buddhist nuns in Burma are called *silashin* or *thilashin*. "Sila" means "moral integrity"; "shin" means "possessor." Therefore, a "silashin" is a possessor of moral integrity. The silashin usually follows eight precepts, has her head shaved and wears a long-sleeved pinkish blouse and brown robe. At Daw Nya na Siri Kyawn Dai Nunnery, the silashins follow nine precepts, the ninth being "to spread loving-kindness to everyone."[4] In this particular nunnery, they accept only girls who have never been married, hoping to maintain the high standard of the nunnery school.

The Sagaing hills on the west bank of Irrawaddy River near Mandalay are famous for their multitude of silashin nunneries. There are 145 nunneries with over 2,000 silashins. It has been recently reported that the ordination ceremony is becoming more elaborate, and that the number of parents who send their daughters to nunnery schools during holidays for short periods (seven days or a month) is on the increase. However, in many nunneries the ceremony involves only shaving one's head and changing into robes. In fact there seems to be no real rules for ordination. In some cases, many monks (up to ten) may be invited, yet in other cases there may be only one monk present. The candidate recites the precepts and is initiated by the monk. It has been pointed out that although the ordination ceremony has little religious significance, the women become real nuns in the course of everyday discipline and study.

Daw Su Su Sein gave a different picture of the process of ordination in the Sagaing area. She reported that if a woman wishes to be ordained, she must go through a preparatory period of at least three months' probation practicing the eight precepts and engaging in meditation. The candidate herself is required to render a promise that she will perform all the duties imposed upon her once admitted. All nuns are expected to abide by at least eight precepts, with the option to undertake nine or ten precepts if they choose.[5]

Some nunneries are better than others in education. Daw Nya na Siri Kyawn Dai is regarded as one of the best nunneries in Burma because its students have been producing very good results in the national exams. In 1986, there were 200 silashins with fifteen silashin teachers at the national exams. For several years, the highest scoring student in the country has been from this nunnery.[6]

The Ven. Dhammadinna described a nunnery established by Daw Panna as a school for silashins with approximately thirty residents, some between the ages of six and twelve, the majority teenagers below the age of twenty-two. The school follows the curriculum dictated by the requirements of the exam, but Daw Panna seems to have the autonomy to set the tone and emphasis of her own nunnery towards Dharma discourses and the practice of meditation.[7]

The discipline of the more organized nunneries entails attendance at morning and evening chanting. The silashins usually rise at 5 a.m. to attend the morning chanting, cook and eat breakfast, and then follow this either with meditation or studying the texts. These may be considered the principle activities of silashins.

In the late afternoon, after classes, they attend to manual work, for example, drawing water or changing the offerings of flowers. Around 6 p.m. they gather for evening chanting, and listen to Dharma talks. Before *uposatha* days, the full moon confessional ceremony, the grounds of the nunnery are cleaned. The silashins are vegetarians and try to remain helpful to others in all their tasks.[8]

Young girls who have left their homes to join the nunneries are under the direct care of their silashin teachers. The relationship between them is like that of parent and child. The elder silashin will
not only teach but care for her students in many other ways.

The life of a Burmese silashin includes an early education in
studying the teachings of the Buddha. As they grow older, the
silashins practice meditation and other devotional practices. They
do not become involved in political activities or discussion. Their
religious life is one of recitation, Dharma talks, and studies. The
silashins of Burma nurture a tranquil life apart from worldly life.

NEPAL

Lumbini, in Nepal, is the historical birthplace of the Buddha, but
the history of Buddhism in modern Nepal began only sixty years ago,
when a group of Nepalese men accepted ordination from Burmese
monks who were visiting Nepal on their way from Kushinagar, where
the Buddha passed away. At that time, five Nepalese women also
came forward to receive the precepts. In Nepal, the history of the
Buddhist ordination of men and women is linked.

Buddhist nuns in Nepal are called *anagarikas,* meaning those who
have left household lives. They are also often respectfully addressed
as *gurumas.* "Guru" means "teacher," and "ma" is an honorific suffix
meaning "mother," thus the term gives the sense of a caring mother
who also teaches Dharma. Anagarikas follow the tradition of the
Burmese, wearing the same long-sleeved blouses with brown robes
usually folded on their left shoulder. They observe ten precepts, but
replace the traditional precept on "not handling money" with the
precept "to have loving-kindness for all living beings."[9]

Since women were not allowed access to education during the
Rana autocracy (1846-1950), most Nepalese nuns are uneducated
and many are elderly. Ven. Dhammawati (born 1927) reported that
it is only in her generation that nuns have started to be ordained at
an early age. Dhammawati is a prominent nun in Nepal, and the following sketch of her life and activities will give a picture of the situation of Nepalese nuns.

At the age of fourteen, Dhammawati traveled to Burma in search
of Dharma education, as it was not available in Nepal. Because of

her young age, her parents refused to give her permission to go, so she ran away from home. She walked to Burma and she was arrested for entering the country illegally. Finally she was able to get a passport and to study as planned.

Dhammawati spent fourteen years studying Dharma, specializing in the *Abhidharma*. Returning to Nepal in 1955, she was determined to work for the propagation of Dharma and for the advancement of women. By 1966 she had succeeded in establishing a nunnery called Dharmakirti Vihar, in Kathmandu, where there are now fourteen nuns studying and practicing. In addition to study and practice, the nuns at Dharmakirti Vihar also engage in teaching and various other Dharma activities. The vihar is supported by laypeople, and every uposatha day, about nine hundred lay disciples, mostly women, attend the Buddha *puja* (offering ceremony).

The main objectives of Dharmakirti Vihar are to preach Theravada Buddhism to lay Buddhists, to elevate the status of women through various activities, to provide Buddhist education for children, and to encourage young people to study Buddhism and put it into practice in their daily lives. The activities of the center include organizing meditation sessions and arranging trips to the places of Buddhist interest in Nepal and neighboring countries.

A Buddha puja, consisting of prayers and offerings, is held at the vihar five times a month, and there is also a Dharma talk. At the end of the service lay Buddhists make offerings to the nuns. Two women members of the vihar are selected to tell stories from the *Jatakas* to the audience. A quiz contest based on Buddhism is often held.

Every Sunday, the vihar runs a religious class for young children. Prizes from a donated fund are awarded at the end of each year to three children selected on the basis of their understanding of their studies. Dharmakirti Bauddha Adhyayan Gosthi is an organization for Buddhist studies started by Dhammawati in 1972. In addition to the meditation sessions held at the vihar, meditation camps at various places have been held under the guidance of Burmese nuns visiting Nepal.[10]

At present there are about sixty nunneries in Nepal. Most Nepalese nuns live alone or in small groups. About half of these women are elderly; the remainder are younger and working hard to establish the Dharma. The Ven. Dhammawati pointed out that there is a great need for an organization that will unite, coordinate, and strengthen the activities of Nepalese nuns. In February 1987, the Ven. Dhammawati participated in the International Conference on Buddhist Nuns in India, and in November 1988 she received higher ordination as a bhikkhuni at Hsi Lai Temple near Los Angeles along with a few of her followers. These women form the nucleus of the Bhikkhuni Sangha in Nepal.

CHINA

Dr. Hema Goonatilake, a Sri Lankan Buddhist scholar who visited China in 1984, reports that prior to the Cultural Revolution, it was generally accepted that there were about 500,000 temples and three million monks and nuns in China.[11] The suppression of Buddhism began as early as 1920, and many temples and nunneries were converted into barracks, factories, warehouses, and public schools. Monks and nuns, especially the younger ones, were forced to disrobe and take jobs in schools, vegetarian restaurants, and the like. Following the fall of the Gang of Four, the repression of Buddhism has noticeably lessened, and some Buddhist temples are being restored.

Dr. Goonatilake visited Zi Xiu, one of the largest nunneries in Shanghai, which had been recently opened to visitors for the first time in eighteen years. The nunnery was founded a century ago, and four generations of nuns have since lived there. During the Cultural Revolution, the nunnery was turned into a warehouse and the nuns were compelled to work in factories or were sent to the countryside to farm. The older ones, who restored the nunnery, said proudly that they practiced the Dharma while living in their countryside homes and growing their own food. At the time of Goonatilake's visit, the oldest of the fifteen who returned was eighty-six and in fragile health. The abbess was seventy-three and had been a nun since the age of twenty. The nun who was a teacher and the head of the training school was seventy-nine.

Of the twenty-six nuns residing in the nunnery, eleven had entered the order after the nunnery was restored in 1982. Their ages ranged from thirteen to twenty-eight. They all came from farming or working-class families, and had been strongly influenced by deeply religious parents and grandparents. Three among them had close connections with the Buddhist clergy; one nun's aunt was a nun; another had two brothers who were monks; the third had been brought up by a nun.

The nuns at the school are given a two-year training course, consisting primarily of the study of Buddhist texts, Chinese language, Chinese history, and meditation. Dr. Goonatilake also observed the nuns' religious activities and their interactions with the lay community. Occasionally, laypeople come to the temple to chant, pray, and speak with the nuns. The temple is very crowded on holidays.

Besides this nunnery, Dr. Goonatilake visited two others in Nanjing and Beijing. Both nunneries are in the process of being restored, with nineteen nuns in residence in the former and only six in the latter. The abbess in each place is in her seventies. Religious activities are similar in both nunneries.

Dr. Goonatilake noticed deep enthusiasm in the monks and nuns she encountered at Chinese temples and nunneries. Although the temples run by monks appeared to be better patronized and organized, some Buddhist temples she visited in Beijing, Nanjing, Shanghai, and Canton held religious ceremonies that were well attended by both men and women. What was of significant concern, however, was the low participation of young devotees. Chinese people born after the Cultural Revolution seem to have less commitment to religion and lack appreciation of religious values. The Chinese Buddhists are aware of this, and are trying to recruit young people.

The reintroduction of Buddhist nuns in China was discussed in a brief article by Prof. Jan Yun-hua.[12] Originally from Ssuchuan, Prof. Yun-hua visited China in 1981 and 1983. He reported that in 1983, a training center for Buddhist women had been founded at Ch'eng-tu Temple in Fuchow. Thirty-three women were recruited from various provinces for training. The age of the trainees was between twenty and thirty, all had completed high school, and each passed an entrance examination for the Buddhist education program.

Another school for Buddhist nuns was established in Ssuchuan in 1983. Admission to this school is restricted to high school graduates between the ages of eighteen and twenty-five. The study program takes two years, with a certificate and rank in the religious profes-

*only in Taiwan is
Bhikkuni Sangha
larger + more influential
than Bhikkhu Sangha*

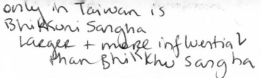

Buddhist Nuns in Other Countries

sion being awarded to those who pass a final examination.

At the Ch'eng-tu training center, the first group of trainees consisted of fifty women ranging in age between eighteen and forty. Admission into the training center requires a high school diploma, a recommendation from a local Buddhist association, and an entrance examination. The subjects covered in the exam include general knowledge of Buddhism and Chinese culture, plus the ability to read and write Chinese. Those who wish to become professional nuns must obtain the consent of their families in advance.

There have also been attempts to revive the Chinese ordination lineage. In 1982, twenty-one new nuns were ordained at Ch'eng-tu Temple. The ceremony was conducted according to the traditional regulations, in which the nuns received ordination first from the bhikkhunis and then from the bhikkhus. This is the first known ordination of nuns in China in the last thirty years.

In 1983, there was a large ordination of Buddhist monks and nuns at Nan-hua Temple in Kwangtung province. There were 250 monks and nuns from Shensi, Honan, Kuangsi, Hunan, and Kuang-tung provinces who received full ordination before the Triple Assembly: the novice precepts, the bhikkhu and bhikkhuni precepts, and the bodhisattva precepts. It is generally believed that in 1982 the number of Buddhist monks and nuns in China, including Tibetan and Mongolian *lamas* (masters), was around 25,000. Most of these were elderly men and women. Ordinations over the last few years are probably fewer than 1,000. The number of Buddhist professionals in China in the future will be substantially fewer than today.

TAIWAN

Taiwan, another unique country in the history of Buddhist nuns, is now a stronghold of the Bhikkhuni Sangha. Taiwan is the only country in the Buddhist world where the Bhikkhuni Sangha is larger than the Bhikkhu Sangha. One of Taiwan's most prominent senior monks once declared publicly that Buddhist education in Taiwan is in the hands of the bhikkhunis.

Buddhism was introduced into Taiwan as early as the twelfth century, but in the absence of written records not much can be said about the development of Taiwanese Buddhism in its early period.

higher education
opportunities
for nuns in Taiwan
⇒ med/law school THAI WOMEN IN BUDDHISM

According to the Ven. Bhikkhuni Shih Yung Kai, Buddhism suffered considerably during the Japanese occupation of 1895-1945.[13] In the Chinese Buddhist tradition, monks and nuns observe strict vegetarianism and celibacy, but under Japanese influence these rules were suspended.

After the Second World War, Taiwan became the seat of the national Chinese government when the Communist Party took power on the mainland. Many senior monks settled in Taiwan, and the presence of these monks revived and enriched Buddhism there and helped clear away the confusion created by the Japanese occupation. At the same time, the renewed leadership of the Sangha encouraged Buddhists to participate in social work with a positive attitude.

The Buddhist Association of the Republic of China (BAROC) was formed in Taiwan in 1950, a continuation of an earlier association in Mainland China. At present, there are 2,000 temples and organizations, most of which were built after 1950. Thirty-four of these temples have affiliated institutes for Sangha training, and over ten of them have Buddhist colleges, all of which provide education for both monks and nuns. Other institutions of higher education, such as ordinary colleges and universities, do not place any restrictions on the admission of monks and nuns. There are examples of nuns who have successfully completed studies in medical colleges and law schools.

In 1952, the first "Triple Altar Ordination" was initiated by the BAROC. The first of three levels of ordination is the *sramanera* and *sramanerika* (Pali: *samanera* and *samaneri*) ordination which is usually given after two weeks of training. A week later, the bhikkhu or bhikkhuni ordination is given. The bodhisattva ordination is given during the last two days of the proceedings. The bodhisattva precepts are contained in the *Brahmajala Sutra*.

From this beginning, over 10,000 monks and nuns have been ordained in Taiwan, 6-7,000 of whom are nuns. Of these, half are between twenty and forty years of age. Presently, nuns in Taiwan have the same opportunities and responsibilities as monks in terms of studying and teaching Dharma. The population of nuns is distributed among the 2,000 temples; in most there are twenty to thirty nuns, and a like number of monks. There are only a few large

great influence
of Taiwanese
bhikkhunis

importance of & education
is being realized among
bhikkhunis in Taiwan

Buddhist Nuns in Other Countries

temples with more than 200 monks and nuns in residence.

There are two modes of living for nuns in a temple. The first involves study in a Buddhist college affiliated with the temple. Students are usually novices or newly ordained monks and nuns. The educational program normally takes three years and includes Buddhist history and philosophy, as well as foreign language study and other non-Buddhist subjects. Others who do not choose to study in university lead a monastic life in the temple of their choice. Activities and practices differ from temple to temple.

The most immediate concern of the monks and nuns in all temples is economic stability, and there are different means of achieving this. Some temple communities are completely self-reliant, supporting themselves by growing their own food and providing their own daily necessities, while others perform prayers and chanting for devotees who make offerings in exchange for this service, usually in the form of money. Going for alms is not generally accepted in Chinese society.

Taiwanese nuns engage in various types of Dharma work—giving public lectures on Buddhism, social work, operating kindergartens, organizing retreats, and teaching in high schools, Buddhist colleges, and universities. Some are also involved in cultural activities such as editing and publishing Buddhist books and magazines. Their principal support comes from private donations from devotees. The main communal religious activity for nuns living in a temple is morning and evening chanting. In addition, nuns do individual practices on their own, such as reciting the names of the Buddha, making prostrations, chanting sutras, and practicing meditation. Seven-day retreats are held throughout the year. Various other Dharma functions and ceremonies are organized for special occasions.

An ordinary bhikkhuni in Taiwan today has at least a primary education, and most have finished high school or college before entering the Sangha. More bhikkhunis are realizing the importance of education, and in recent years, many have traveled to Japan, Korea, India, and the United States to continue their education.

From the activities and accomplishments of bhikkhunis in Taiwan today, we can see that they are assuming a very important and influential role in the religious sector as well as in society as a whole. If the trend of young women entering the Sangha continues, adding new talent and energy to the monastic community, the Bhikkhuni Sangha in Taiwan has the potential to become a very powerful force for social and spiritual health.

KOREA

Buddhism was transmitted to Korea from China in the fourth century. The ordination of nuns was introduced soon after the ordination of monks. Korean monasteries are strictly separated by gender. Members live a communal lifestyle, with little privacy or personal property. Monks and nuns have their robes and little else.

The Ven. Karma Lekshe Tsomo, who received ordination in a Korean lineage, offers the following account of monastic life in a Korean temple.[14] Work around the monastery or nunnery is shared on a rotation basis. Senior residents are usually engaged in administrative responsibilities rather than in manual labor. As in ancient China, large monasteries in Korea continue to grow their own food. They provide most of their own vegetables, and some grains, although grain is also offered by the lay community. All the daily needs of the monks and nuns are taken care of by the monastery, so there is no need to go out to find work or to earn a livelihood. The work around the monastery keeps everyone very busy.

The practice of meditation is strongly emphasized in the Korean Buddhist tradition. There are currently over 500 nuns practicing intensive meditation in meditation halls throughout Korea, and 40 nuns are engaged in three-year retreats. During the summer and winter retreat seasons, the monks and nuns live in the meditation halls. Once the retreat has begun, one is committed to staying until the end of the session. A nun can choose to attend a retreat in some other monastery where there is a good meditation master. Song Kwang Sa, a monastery in southern Korea, is particularly famous due to its late master Kusan Sunim.

The daily routine is fairly standard. In urban temples, the rising time is usually 4 a.m., while in rural temples 3 a.m. is the norm. The monks and nuns congregate for a short session of chanting and prostrations. Breakfast is at 6 a.m., followed by cleaning the temple. In the Zen tradition, all actions are considered Dharma activities.

young people drawn to monastic life in KOREA *higher ed. for ♀*

Lunch and dinner are served at 11 a.m. and 5 p.m., respectively. There is a chanting period before lunch. As in the Chinese tradition, all meals are vegetarian, but onion and garlic are excluded from the diet. Between meals, residents attend to their particular activities, whether work, study, or meditation.

In recent years the number of young people drawn to monastic life has increased. There are an average of 200 nuns at the annual bhikkhuni ordination. The completion of a high school education is required for ordination. All monks and nuns attend a Buddhist temple for three to five years, where they study Chinese language and learn Buddhist sutras. At an institute for nuns in Unmun Sa in central Korea, nuns spend four years in training, with intensive study in the sutras and *Vinaya*. A Buddhist women's college in Seoul provides an educational facility for nuns. Teachers in this college are monks and nuns, as well as professors from other universities.

There are currently about 6,000 bhikkhunis and sramanerikas in Korea, and a large number of women in training. A woman must complete a minimum of five years of vigorous training before she can apply for ordination. Ordination is now nationalized; rather than receiving ordination on an individual basis, the disciples of different masters from all over Korea meet once a year to receive ordination at a chosen site, which changes every few years. Candidates receive uniform training in discipline, deportment, and *Vinaya*, in addition to receiving the vows of higher ordination. This system has greatly improved the standards of discipline within the Korean Sangha.

During the Japanese occupation (1909-1945), some Korean monks followed the Japanese tradition which allows monks to marry, resulting in the decline of the monastic school. Lacking political and economic support, the monks and nuns had to struggle to keep their monasteries going. Nevertheless, the monastic tradition was preserved and both the bhikkhu and bhikkhuni lineages have survived. In 1981, the Chogye Order, the leading monastic order in Korea, reintroduced the dual ordination procedure.

JAPAN

Japan received Buddhism from China in the sixth century. There are many schools of Buddhism in Japan, but the two most prevalent

monks allowed to marry /
nuns must remain celibate

sects are Zen, which emphasizes meditation practice, and Pure Land, which emphasizes devotional practices and faith in Amitabha Buddha. The Rev. Tessho Kondo reported that there are about 2,000 Zen nuns in half as many temples.[15] In the Pure Land sect, there are 700 nuns in 500 temples. Most nuns live alone and carry full responsibility as the head priests of temples. Many nuns are over sixty years old, and young successors are very few. Because of smaller families in modern society, parents tend to allow only sons to follow the path. And to answer to hereditary requirements, monks are allowed to marry and have a family, while nuns must maintain celibacy and thus do not pass on the family lineage.

A point of distinction in Japanese Buddhism is that Japanese "nuns" and "monks" are not the same as those in other Buddhist traditions, but are closer to priests or "ministers of religion." The nuns maintain the bodhisattva precepts. Historically, Japanese women received bhikkhuni ordination in Korea as early as the year 590, but there were only three bhikkhunis present, which did not meet the minimum number of five required by tradition. Thus, the bhikkhuni lineage was not established. In 754, three Chinese nuns came to Japan but could not transmit the lineage due to the lack of a Bhikkhuni Sangha, with the result that a proper Bhikkhuni Sangha has never been established in Japan.[16]

Many courses are offered in the formal training schools, with the primary focus placed on each particular sect's way to enlightenment: *nembutsu* (recitation of the name of Amitabha Buddha) in the Pure Land schools and *zazen* (sitting meditation) in the Zen schools. Other subjects may include Buddhist history and philosophy, sutra study, instruction and practice in ceremonies, sewing of priests' robes, and instruction in the Zen-related arts of the tea ceremony, flower arrangement, and calligraphy.

Upon completion of training, a nun is certified to perform all the ceremonies of her tradition and to become head priest of a temple. Each temple is an independent legal entity. The livelihood of the head priest depends on the temple's supporters. This means that the primary duties of the head priest are those required by the laypeople who support the temple. In this regard, a less clearly defined but often more time-consuming duty is counseling the lay supporters of the temple, offering advice and guidance with the many problems of everyday life. The life of a Japanese nun is thus a very busy and fulfilling one, and she is very close to the community of which she is a part, even though she usually lives separately from her fellow nuns.

TIBET

As reported by Ven. Lobsang Dechen, Buddhism reached Tibet in the seventh century during the reign of King Songtsen Gampo.[17] The first monastery, for monks only, was founded in the eighth century, and the first nunnery was established in Phenpo, north of Lhasa, the capital of Tibet.

Among the many celebrated female practitioners of Tibet were a large number of nuns. The isolated settings of the nunneries provided an environment conducive to intensive religious practice, and the earnestness of the nuns in their spiritual endeavors was greatly appreciated by the lay community.

Prior to 1959, when China invaded and occupied the country, Tibet was home to one of the largest communities of Buddhist nuns in the world. There were 618 nunneries with 7,141 nuns in the Nyingma sect; 6,831 nuns of the Gelug sect; 3,697 Kagyu nuns; and 1,159 of the Sakya sect; for a total of 12,398 Buddhist nuns in Tibet. Forty-four nunneries were quite large, housing more than 100 nuns each. During the period of Chinese rule in Tibet, the Buddhist community has suffered greatly and most monastic institutions have been totally destroyed. During the 1960s, not a single robed figure could be seen anywhere in Tibet.

Fortunately, prior to the decimation of Tibet by China, the Tibetan tradition had spread widely in neighboring Asian countries. In India there are approximately 339 Tibetan nuns in Ladakh, 250 in Zanskar, 100 in Lahaul, 103 in Spiti, and 106 in Kinnaur. In Bhutan, there are 600 Tibetan nuns. Many other young women wish to become nuns and join nunneries, but they are unable to do so because of limited accommodations.

More recently the Tibetan tradition has taken root in many Western countries. There is one Tibetan nunnery in France, called Dorje Pamo, with five nuns. There are another 240 Western women ordained in the Tibetan tradition settled in various countries. The

*Tibetan tradition
has spread int'lly* (handwritten)

present Tibetan nuns are not fully ordained, however, having received only the sramanerika ordination. In 1984, four Tibetan nuns received full ordination in Hong Kong. In 1988, more Western nuns in the Tibetan tradition received bhikkhuni ordination at Hsi Lai Temple in Los Angeles.

There is evidence that, beginning in the twelfth century, a few great lamas did give the bhikkhuni vows to Tibetan women but without the assistance of bhikkhunis, and the validity of the transmission is thus disputed. From the Theravada standpoint, which holds that the ordination of a bhikkhuni requires the presence of both Sanghas, the Tibetan bhikkhuni ordination is not valid. Nevertheless, the fact remains that in Tibet's history, there were Tibetan masters who gave full ordination to women.[18]

A look at a nunnery in Tibet will provide a better understanding of Tibetan nuns.[19] There were many nunneries of each school which enjoyed recognition and where many famous nuns reached a high level of realization. These women affected the lives of many others through their advanced spiritual development.

Nechung Ri Nunnery dates back to the early fifteenth century. It was built in the traditional Tibetan style, with the main temple in the middle of the compound, surrounded by living and administrative quarters. The whole nunnery was set in a deep, peaceful forest. Traditional life in the nunnery began with the senior nuns teaching newly ordained women to read and write. This was followed by sutra study, the memorization of prayers and sacred chants, training in the proper observance of religious ceremonies, and in playing such instruments as cymbals, trumpets, and drums, which were used during ceremonies. Lamas were invited to give scriptural teachings to the nuns.

The nuns also performed ceremonies at the request of the community and had a special reputation for their Tara rituals. All the nuns, within the limit of their abilities, took turns in holding the various offices, from housekeeper to head nun, so that in due course most of them had trained in everything necessary to run a nunnery.

Given the political disturbances in Tibet, any proper current picture of Tibetan nuns cannot be limited to Tibet alone. It is worthwhile to look at some existing Tibetan nunneries in other countries.

The Ven. Kunga reported that His Holiness the Gyalwa Karmapa of the Kagyu sect established a nunnery called Karma Chokhor Dechen at Rumtek monastery in Sikkim, India.[20] This project, begun in 1983, now houses eighteen nuns ranging in age from ten to sixty-five. At present, the young ordainees learn to read the religious texts and to perform all the rituals necessary for their daily meditation and devotions, as well as for offering prayers for patrons. Future plans include constructing facilities for the nuns to study Buddhist philosophy and quarters for undertaking extended meditation retreats.

Ven. Karma Lekshe Tsomo has pointed out that Geden Chöling, in Dharamsala, India, is probably the largest functioning nunnery of the Tibetan tradition in the world, since most of the nunneries in Tibet itself have been destroyed.[21] Nearly eighty nuns belong to Geden Chöling, but due to lack of adequate accommodation, only sixty live in the nunnery itself. The rest live with relatives in the surrounding villages and join the others for pujas and teachings.

The majority of nuns at Geden Chöling are Tibetan, though not necessarily from Tibet. With the excellent study program at this nunnery and its proximity to His Holiness the Dalai Lama's residence, and access to his teachings and blessings, dozens of nuns from neighboring areas are anxious to gain admission but are prevented due to the limited facilities.

The residents of Geden Chöling are mostly under thirty. Due to lack of accommodation, admission has been limited to those in the lower age bracket in order to see them through the educational process. The nuns began to take an active interest in pursuing a monastic curriculum about three years ago. They took the initiative to invite someone to teach them the basic logic texts. Though these texts are very technical and profound, and generally their study has been deemed the prerogative of male scholars, the nuns have shown tremendous aptitude and great enthusiasm in this field of learning.

Another Tibetan nunnery, Jangchub Chöling, was founded in 1985 in Mundgod, a town in South India. The Ven. Jampa Tsedroen (Carola Roloff) reported that during her visit the prayer hall for the nunnery was already completed.[22] About twenty sramanerikas from different schools of the Tibetan tradition and twenty young novices, most of whom received the tonsure from His Holiness the Dalai

Lama, meet there regularly for pujas. The nunnery is headed by the Ven. Thubten Lhatso (in 1987, age forty-five) who had recently come from Tibet. The senior nuns are very enthusiastic and welcome the many important changes that are envisioned. They are eager to give their support for a new generation of nuns, and to improve educational opportunities, and they anticipate the establishment of the Bhikkhuni Sangha. The nunnery is receiving active support from the Tibetan Women's Association and the Tibetan movement's representatives in Mundgod.

Tibetan Buddhist Nuns, by Hanna Havnevik, published by the Norwegian University Press, provides much more detail about Tibetan nuns. It is the most complete research work on this topic to date.

VIETNAM, LAOS, AND CAMBODIA

Due to prolonged political disturbances in Vietnam, Laos, and Cambodia, not much recent information is available on Buddhist communities in these countries. Five Cambodian women have been sponsored to attend the 1991 conference on Buddhist nuns in Bangkok. Two are nuns, and we hope to learn more from these women about the situation in Cambodia. The Cambodian nuns wear white robes, and are similar to Thai mae jis.

WESTERN COUNTRIES

The number of Western Buddhist women asking for ordination has been on the increase. In the past two decades many Western Buddhist nuns have appeared in various traditions throughout the world. The spread of Buddhism in the West has opened up a new era for women's spiritual development. A number of Western women who have accepted Buddhism are more committed to join the order and lead the lives of samaneris and bhikkhunis than some who were born into a Buddhist tradition.

In the United States, most Buddhist traditions are represented, including Tibetan, Chinese, Japanese, Korean, Vietnamese, Sri Lankan, Thai, Cambodian, and Laotian. With the exception of the last three, there are Western nuns in all of these traditions. In the Tibetan tradition only sramanerika ordination is available, so West-

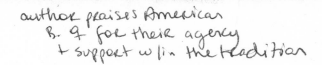
author praises American B. Q for their agency + support w/in the tradition

ern nuns who have received this ordination will have to wait a minimum of two years before they can apply for higher ordination, which usually takes place in Taiwan. Thereafter, they continue to practice and follow their Tibetan teachers' instruction. This is partly due to the strong teacher-student relationship characteristic of the Tibetan tradition, and partly due to language barriers with their Chinese preceptors and teachers.

There are also cases of Western women who took lower ordination in Sri Lanka and later became bhikkhunis in the Chinese lineage. Ven. Miao Kwang Sudharma, an American woman who received full ordination in Taiwan in 1984, maintains her ordained names from both traditions. Ven. Ayya Khema, a German woman who received full ordination at Hsi Lai Temple in Los Angeles in 1988, prefers her Theravadin name, and wears the brown robe of Theravadin tradition.

Chinese ordination is the most authentic lineage available at this time, and Taiwan is its stronghold. Many more women than men attend the annual ordination ceremony. Women with lower ordination from other traditions seek higher ordination in Taiwan. Previously, Western nuns had to travel to Taiwan to receive ordination in the Chinese lineage. Western nuns seeking higher ordination can now go to Hsi Lai Temple, a branch of Fo Kwang Shan in Taiwan, in Hacienda Heights, near Los Angeles, California.

In 1988, an international ordination was organized at Hsi Lai Temple and more than 200 women received the bhikkhuni ordination. This is the first time in Buddhist history that such ordination has been provided on such a large scale in a non-Buddhist country. Women from the U.S., Canada, England, Thailand, Sri Lanka, and Nepal participated in this auspicious event, ordaining in the Tibetan, Vietnamese, Korean, Japanese, and Chinese traditions.

Anyone who has studied Western Buddhism cannot help but notice the uniqueness of women's participation in American Buddhism. American Buddhist women are not only supportive, but also assertive in the role they play in Buddhism. The leadership of any Buddhist tradition putting down roots in North America must acknowledge the strong participation of women. Coming from relative isolation in their home countries, the monks of all traditions are forced to be more realistic about the spiritual needs of Buddhist women in the Western context.

Theravadin monks are slowly coming around to this realization. Sri Lankan monks, though still not in unity, are now beginning to offer samaneri ordination with the help of foreign bhikkhunis to Asian women. This process will lead slowly to the ordination of bhikkhunis in the Theravadin tradition and eventually bring about the revival of the Bhikkhuni Sangha in the Theravadin lineage.

Gampo Abbey in Nova Scotia is a *Vinaya* training center for monks and nuns in the Tibetan tradition, headed by an American bhikkhuni, the Ven. Ane Pema Chodron. There are many other Buddhist traditions active in Canada, particularly in the Toronto area, where the Buddhist population doubled in 1988.

Bhikkhunis and samaneris can now be found all over Europe. Buddhist nuns may even be found in Poland, where the Ven. Nisatta, a Swedish bhikkhuni, carries out a regular Dharma program of chanting and meditation in her small apartment. In South Africa and even in the U.S.S.R., small groups of Buddhist men and women are forming and organizing Dharma meetings on a regular basis, although these groups do not yet have Buddhist nuns.

In West Germany, the Ven. Jampa Tsedroen, a German bhikkhuni in the Tibetan tradition, is active in running a Tibetan meditation center. She helped to organize the 1987 international conference on Buddhist nuns and is currently working towards the 1991 international conference on Buddhist women to be held in Thailand.

The Ven. Bhikkhuni Ayya Khema has started meditation centers both in Australia and West Germany, and travels annually between West Germany, Sri Lanka, and Australia to lead retreats and give Dharma talks.[23]

In England, the Ven. Sumedho, an American monk ordained in Thailand, has established two Buddhist meditation centers.[24] He has also been giving ordination to brown-robed Western nuns following the ten precepts. Also in England, the Friends of Western Buddhist Order (FWBO) led by the Ven. Sangharakshita, provides a separate group for Buddhist women called *dharmacarinis*, who are active in forming their own centers of Buddhist practice and meditation.

Sakyadhita, the International Association of Buddhist Women, also has members in England. Sakyadhita England had its first meeting in September 1989 and is planning its third annual meeting.[25]

In Australia, the Ven. Khantipalo, an English monk ordained in the Thai tradition, is giving the ten precepts to Buddhist nuns at his monastery at Wat Buddha Dhamma.[26] There are also one or two Tibetan Buddhist centers in Australia, where Western Buddhist nuns are active with Dharma engagements.

One hundred twenty Buddhist nuns, monks, and laywomen from all over the world participated in the 1987 International Conference on Buddhist Nuns at Bodh Gaya, India. The result of this conference was the formation of Sakyadhita, an International Association of Buddhist Women. The conference was coordinated by Sister Ayya Khema, Bhikkhuni Karma Lekshe Tsomo, and myself. The following resolutions were formulated:

> Whereas, although our specific practices and lineages may vary, we are all sisters and brothers in the Buddha Dharma and share a common source, and
>
> Whereas Buddhist women wish to improve themselves and take their just and equal opportunity and responsibility in society, and
>
> Whereas there is convened at Bodh Gaya, India, the place of Lord Buddha's enlightenment, a Conference on Buddhist Nuns from many countries around the world,
>
> We, therefore, resolve that on this 16th day of February 1987, we establish SAKYADHITA, World-wide Buddhist Women, an international organization formed to assist Buddhist women around the world.
>
> It is further resolved that an interim executive committee begin effecting the establishment of such an organization, and
>
> It is further resolved that the goals of this organization shall be to:
>
> 1. Foster world peace for all sentient beings.
>
> 2. Work in harmony with all Buddhist Sanghas, traditions and communities.
>
> 3. Establish and promote harmonious understanding with other religious communities.
>
> 4. Hold conferences and seminars on Buddhist women's issues.

5. Establish a system of communication between Buddhist women all over the world.

6. Research into women's role in the Buddha Dharma.

7. Improve education for Buddhist women (general and Dharma).

8. Encourage and improve Buddhist practice for nuns and laywomen.

9. Educate and train women as teachers of Buddha Dharma.

10. Preserve the teaching and make it available throughout the world.

11. Research into the *Vinaya* of the different traditions.

12. Establish an international Bhikkhuni Sangha organization.

13. Introduce samaneri (female novice), sikkhamana (female practitioner), and bhikkhuni ordinations where they currently do not exist.

14. Provide help and assistance to Buddhist nuns and those who wish to receive ordination.

15. Establish committees to carry out the organization's goals.

16. Set up bylaws, a constitution, and effect registration of the organization.

As it stands, the administrative body of the Association has not yet been very effective, due to the fact that the committee members live far apart. At the 1991 conference on Buddhist women mentioned previously, members will meet to develop strategies to overcome this problem.

An international organization such as Sakyadhita can be an important symbol of Buddhist women's unity and a forum for achieving creative and constructive goals. In the long run, this organization aims at helping to support recently formed nuns' communities all over the world. The organization can be tapped to provide human resources to fill the gap in various countries, especially at the early formative stages of Buddhist women's communities, and can also help to provide training for Buddhist nuns, so that they become strong in their spiritual development and provide effective spiritual guidance to society.

importance of int'l B. organizations
as symbol of unity

* * * * *

This is the conclusion of the book, but definitely not the end of the issue. Changes and improvements can be expected.

The purpose of this book has been to inform the reader and to encourage concerned scholars and engaged Buddhists to pursue further study and action. I hope that the publication of this book will mark the end of the "closed door" attitude towards women's full participation in Buddhism in Thailand and elsewhere. Using the materials presented here, women should take a positive stand regarding their own attitudes towards themselves and the world.

Buddhism is a beautiful, vital religion. Its teaching liberates and accommodates everyone. Buddhist women should take full advantage of this spirit, and not get bogged down in the negative attitudes still manifested among some ignorant Buddhist authorities and organizations. We must realize the deep-rooted nature of ignorance and counter it only with education, compassion, and understanding. As more and more Buddhist women come together and prove their efficacy and value to society, the issues described in this book will become obsolete. Buddhist women must realize that the task of breaking collective misinterpretations and prejudices solidified into sacred tradition over centuries requires a strong commitment and deep compassion. With perseverance and intelligence, we can rectify the problems and reclaim our spiritual heritage.

---

[1] As material on Buddhist nuns is scarce, I have relied heavily on information found in the book *Sakyadhita: Daughters of the Buddha*, edited by Karma Lekshe Tsomo (Ithaca: Snow Lion Publications, 1988). This book was the result of the first international conference of Buddhist nuns held in Bodh Gaya, India in 1987. It includes the most complete and current information on Buddhist nuns available to date.

[2] C. Mabel Rickmer, trans., "Kakurumahantamana Inscription," in *Cullavamsa* (Colombo: Ceylon Government Information Department, 1953) 42: 68.

[3] Edward Conze, ed., *Buddhist Texts Through The Ages* (Boston: Shambhala, 1990), p. 293.

[4] Hiroko Kawanami, "Buddhist Nuns in Burma," in *NIBWA* no. 9, October-December 1986.

[5] Da Su Su Sein, "Nuns of Burma," in *Sakyadhita: Daughters of the Buddha*, p. 109.

[6] Kawanami, *Op. Cit.*

[7] Ven. Dhammadinna, "Nuns in Burma," in *NIBWA* no. 15, April-June 1988.

8 Da Su Su Sein, *Op. Cit.*, p. 110.

9 Anagarika Dhammawati, "Theravada Nuns of Nepal," in *Sakyadhita: Daughters of the Buddha*, p. 138.

10 Reported in "Dharmakirti Vihar: Nunnery in Nepal," in *NIBWA* no. 9, October-December 1986.

11 Dr. Hema Goonatilake, "Nuns of China: Part I—The Mainland," *Sakyadhita: Daughters of the Buddha*, p. 112.

12 Jan Yua-Hun, "New Ordination of Buddhist Nuns in China," in *NIBWA* no. 6, January-March 1986.

13 Bhiksuni Shih Yung Kai, "Nuns of China: Part II—Taiwan," in *Sakyadhita: Daughters of the Buddha*, p. 119.

14 Bhiksuni Karma Lekshe Tsomo, "Nuns of Korea," in *Sakyadhita: Daughters of the Buddha*, pp. 131-35.

15 Reverend Tessho Kondo, "Nuns of Japan: Part I," in *Sakyadhita: Daughters of the Buddha*, p. 124.

16 Bhiksuni Karma Lekshe Tsomo, "Nuns of Japan: Part II," in *Sakyadhita: Daughters of the Buddha*, p. 129.

17 Sramanerika Lobsang Dechen, "Nuns of Tibet," in *Sakyadhita: Daughters of the Buddha*, p. 150.

18 Acharya Tashi Tsering, "Buddhist Nuns in Tibet," from *Cho-Yang*, Vol. 1, no. 1, reprinted in *NIBWA* no. 9, October-December 1988.

19 "Nechung Ri: A Nunnery in Tibet," from "Tibetan Nuns," written by nuns of Geden Chöling Nunnery, in *NIBWA* no. 7, April-June 1986.

20 Ven. Kunga, "Karma Chokhor Dechen: A Nunnery in Sikkim, India," in *NIBWA* no. 5, October-December 1985.

21 Ven. Karma Lekshe Tsomo, "A brief glimpse at Tibetan Refugee Nunneries," in *NIBWA* no. 12, July-September 1987.

22 Ven. Jampa Tsedroen (Carola Roloff), "New Nunnery in Mundgod," in *NIBWA* no. 12, July-September 1987.

23 The addresses of her centers are: 1. Buddhadharma Hermitage, 6 Coldmines Road, P.O. Box 132, Bundadoon, NSW 2578 Australia; 2. Buddha Haus Meditation Und Studienzentrum, e. V. Uttenbuhl, 5, Gruntelhof, 8967 Oy-Mittelburg, West Germany.

24 The addresses are: 1. Chithurst Monastery, Chithurst, Petersfield, Hampshire, GU31 5EU, England; 2. Amaravati, Great Gaddesden, Hemel Hempstead, Hertfordshire, HP1 3BZ, England.

25 Address: Sakyadhita England, 9 Coldwell Court, Donnithorne Ave., Nuneaton, Warks, CV11 4QQ, England.

26 Address: Wat Buddha Dhamma, Ten Mile Hollow, Wisemans Ferry, NSW 2255, Australia.

Bibliography

Allione, Tsultrim. *Women of Wisdom*. Boston: Routledge & Kegan Paul, 1988.

Barnes, Nancy Schuster. "Buddhism," *Women in World Religions*. Arvind Sharma, ed. New York: State University of New York Press, 1987.

Boucher, Sandy. *Turning the Wheel: American Women Creating the New Buddhism*. San Francisco: Harper & Row, 1988.

Carmody, Denise Lardner. *Women and World Religions*. Nashville, Tennessee: Abingdon, 1979.

Carroll, Theodora Foster. *Women, Religion, and Development in the Third World*. New York: Praeger, 1983.

Conze, Edward, ed. *Buddhist Texts Through The Ages*. Boston: Shambhala Publications, Inc., 1990.

Eck, Diana L., and Devaki Jain, eds. *Speaking of Faith: Global Perspectives on Women, Religion, and Social Change*. Philadelphia, Pennsylvania: New Society Publishers, 1987.

Esterik, Penny Van, ed. *Women of Southeast Asia*. Center for Southeast Asia Monograph Series. Dekalb, Illinois: Northern Illinois University Press, 1982.

Falk, Nancy A., and Rita M. Gross, eds. *Unspoken Worlds: Women's Religious Lives in Non-Western Cultures*. New York: Harper and Row, 1980.

Friedman, Lenore. *Meetings With Remarkable Women: Buddhist Teachers in America*. Boston: Shambhala Publications, Inc., 1987.

Galland, China. *Longing for Darkness: Tara and the Black Madonna*. New York: Viking Penguin, 1990.

Gross, Rita M. "Buddhism and Feminism: Toward Their Mutual Transformation," *The Eastern Buddhist*, Kyoto, Vol XIX, No. 2, 1986.

_____., ed. *Beyond Androcentrism: New Essays on Women and Religion*. Missoula, Montana: Scholar's Press for the American Academy of Religion, 1977.

Havnevik, Hanna. *Tibetan Buddhist Nuns*. Oslo: Norwegian University Press, 1991.

Hopkinson, Deborah, Michelle Hill, and Eileen Kiera, eds. *Not Mixing Up Buddhism: Essays on Women and Buddhist Practice*. Fredonia, New York: White Pine Press, 1986.

Horner, I.B. *Women Under Primitive Buddhism: Laywomen and Almswomen*. 1930. Delhi: Motilal Banarsidass, 1975.

Horner, I.B., tr. and ed. *Sacred Books of the Buddhists*. London: Luzac & Co., 1963.

Jordt, Ingrid. "Bhikkhus, Bhikkhunis and the Classical Pali Buddhist Texts," *Crossroads*. Journal of the South and Southeast Asia Studies Department, University of Illinois.

Kabilsingh, Chatsumarn. *A Comparative Study of the Bhikkhuni Patimokkha*. Varanasi: Chaukhamba Orientalia, 1984.

Kajiyama, Yuichi. "Women in Buddhism," *The Eastern Buddhist*, Kyoto, Autumn 1982.

King, Sallie B., tr. *Passionate Journey: The Spiritual Autobiography of Satomi Myodo*. Boston: Shambhala Publications, 1987.

La Loubère, S.D. *The Kingdom of Siam*. Oxford: Oxford University Press, 1986.

Muller, Max, ed. and Hermann Oldenburg, tr. *Sacred Books of the East*. Delhi: Motilal Banarsidass, 1965.

Muller, Max, ed., and T.W. Rhys Davids, tr. *Buddhist Suttas*. Delhi: Motilal Banarsidass, 1965.

Murcott, Susan. *The First Buddhist Women*. Berkeley: Parallax Press, 1991.

Ochs, Carol. *Women and Spirituality*. Totowa, New Jersey: Rowman & Allanheld, 1983.

Paul, Diana Y. *Women in Buddhism: Images of the Feminine in the Mahayana Tradition*. Berkeley: University of California Press, 1985.

Plasgow, Judith, and Joan Arnold Romero, eds. *Women and Religion*. Missoula, Montana: Scholar's Press for the American Academy of Religion, 1974.

Providence and Prostitution: Image and Reality for Women in Buddhist Thailand. London: Change-International Reports, 1980.

Rhys Davids, C.A.F., tr. *The Book of Kindred Sayings*. London: Luzac & Co., 1950.

_____. *Psalms of the Sisters*. Vol. 1 of *Psalms of the Early Buddhists*. London: Pali Text Society, 1948.

Rhys Davids, T.W., ed. *Sacred Books of the Buddhists*. London: Pali Text Society, 1965.

Rickmer, C. Mabel, trans. *Cullavamsa*. Colombo: Ceylon Government Information Department, 1953.

Sidor, Ellen S., ed. *A Gathering of Spirit*. Cumberland, Rhode Island: Primary Point Press, 1987.

Spretnak, Charlene, ed. *The Politics of Women's Spirituality*. Garden City, New York: Anchor Press/Doubleday, 1982.

Tsomo, Karma Lekshe, ed. *Sakyadhita: Daughters of the Buddha*. Ithaca, New York: Snow Lion Publications, 1988.

Wales, Horace Geoffrey Quaritch. *Early Burma—Old Siam*. London: Bernard Quaritch, 1973.

Willis Janice, ed. *Feminine Ground: Essays on Women and Tibet*. Ithaca, New York: Snow Lion Publications, 1989.

Willis, Janice. "Nuns and Benefactresses: The Role of Women in the Development of Buddhism," *Women, Religion and Social Change*. Yvonne Yazbeck Haddad and Ellison Banks Findly, eds. New York: State University of New York Press, 1985.

"Women & Buddhism," Spring Wind-Buddhist Cultural Forum. Vol. 6, Nos. 1-3. Ann Arbor, Michigan: Zen Lotus Society, 1986.

"Women and Buddhism," *Journal of the Zen Mission Society*. Vol. 7, Nos. 1-2. Mt. Shasta, California: Shasta Abbey, 1976.

The Newsletter on International Buddhist Women's Activities
is published four times a year. For a one-year subscription, please
send $10 U.S. to NIBWA, c/o Dr. Chatsumarn Kabilsingh, Faculty
of Liberal Arts, Thammasat University, Bangkok 10200, Thailand.

Sakyadhita, the International Association of Buddhist Women,
was co-founded in 1989 by Chatsumarn Kabilsingh. For a one-year
membership, which includes a newsletter subscription, send $10 to
Sakyadhita, 400 Hobron Lane, #2616, Honolulu, HI 96815.

Parallax Press publishes books and tapes on socially engaged
Buddhism. We hope that doing so will encourage wider understanding of the interdependence between inner peace and peace in
the world. Some of our recent titles include:

The First Buddhist Women, by Susan Murcott

Being Peace, by Thich Nhat Hanh

The Path of Compassion: Writings on Socially Engaged Buddhism,
    edited by Fred Eppsteiner

Worlds in Harmony: Dialogues on Compassionate Action,
    by His Holiness the Dalai Lama

For a copy of our free catalog, please write to:
Parallax Press, P.O. Box 7355, Berkeley, CA 94707, U.S.A.